ADVANCE PRAISE

From the moment I met the team at Streamline, I knew my long-time book dream would become a reality. First, the encouragement to change lives was so powerful. Second, there was the know-how to punch through and complete the task quickly and efficiently. Finally, the complete community of other authors has been MASTERFULLY assembled to continue to inspire and encourage us all.

If someone has a message they want to share with the world and is looking for tremendous, like-minded encouragers in their life, look no further than the team at Streamline.

As Will and Alex always say, "Let's GO!"

– **Dale Alexander, Author of** *"The Talk" (about money): A Young Adult's Guide to the ONE DECISION That Changes Everything*

I cannot say enough good things about Will, Alex, and the entire team from Streamline. They created a path for my success. From the moment I wrote the first words to the day I completed my book cover and launch, I felt empowered and never overwhelmed. This was thanks to the superb organization throughout the process. I had a fantastic editor who made my book SO much better. She helped me get the most out of my content, and it was so comforting to have someone reading my words every step of the way. Honestly, I miss talking to her every day! This team knows their stuff and is an amazing resource for any author!

– **Katie Mullen, Author of** *The Sales Tightrope: A Research-Based Guide to Not Annoying Customers and Still Being a Top Performer*

In my travels, I often met people at the start of their careers, asking for advice. As I shared my life's lessons for guidance, they said, "You should write a book." It was an intimidating undertaking, but the team at Streamline were experienced leaders. Their kindness and support helped me turn a partially developed manuscript into a beautiful story.

For me, success was not to become the next great author but to inspire others for years to come.

> – Kate Buhler, Author of *Inhospitable:*
> *Lessons Learned from a Lifetime in Service*

From the first conversation, I knew the team at Streamline had a genuine interest in me and would be the perfect partner to help get my voice on paper. I reached out to get assistance with writing a book but found so much more. The community of authors and thought leaders that comprise the Streamline family is unlike any other. Come for the book, stay for the family!

> – Mark Martinez, Author of *Hit Your Grand Slam:*
> *Rounding Life's Bases in a Chase for Greatness*

Thank you to the entire Streamline team, who exuded professional excellence and continued encouragement while I embarked on this exciting publishing journey. New to authorship, I appreciated the many lessons learned along the way and the constructive feedback and guidance provided as Streamline cheered me on toward the finish line! Thank you, Annika, for your brilliant editorial expertise. You kept me on task and challenged me to dig deeper. Thank you, Streamline, for the beautiful book I now hold in my hands!

> – Donna Aust, Author of *When Hope Comes:*
> *Discovering God's Character and Our*
> *True Identity through the Book of Ruth*

Working with Streamline has been a game changer for me and my business. Doors have been opened, confidence has been boosted, leaders have been equipped, a new community has been built, and more people every day are "Closing the Trust Gap." One of my most important personal and business decisions has been partnering with Streamline.

> – Cory Scheer, Author of *Closing the Trust*
> *Gap: Taking Action on What Matters Most*
> *for Leaders, Teams, and Organizations*

The Streamline team is a true pleasure to work with! Their process is excellent, but the people make it great. The entire team encouraged me along the way. When I was struggling with my manuscript, my editing partner always had a suggestion or tweak to make it better. She gave me hope when I felt stuck. I highly recommend Streamline to help you get your book to the world!

– Julie Nee, Author of *Mirror Mirror: 5 Reflections to Clear the Fog and Help You Shine*

Working with Streamline to publish *Send Me* was undoubtedly a divine appointment. Will and Alex have built an unshakeable foundation and culture focused on creating impact and developing genuine relationships over merely pursuing profit. My father-in-law passed away unexpectedly while I was writing my book. The Streamline team showed up in many ways to encourage and support our family throughout our grief. At that moment, Streamline proved they are much more than a publishing company. They are a team of highly talented individuals who believe their authors are much more than a transaction. I am forever grateful.

– Evans Duren, Author of *Send Me: Discovering Your Mission Through Work*

My experience working alongside Streamline has been a dream. Their commitment to helping authors bring their best books to life is their top priority, and I could not be happier with how my debut novel turned out. The level of enthusiasm and expertise they bring to the table can be seen in their work. I highly recommend them and plan to work with them again!

– Mary Coe, Author of *The Aliquian Series*

I cannot recommend working with Streamline highly enough. Without their support, I couldn't have written my book so efficiently or achieved such a high level of organization. The process was intimidating, as I'm sure it might seem to you. However, Will and Alex did a fantastic job guiding me through the details and encouraging me that the world needs to hear my story. I had a few health setbacks along the way, but Will and Alex were patient and understanding. My book turned out fantastic. If you wonder if your story is important enough to share, the answer is yes. I highly recommend working with Streamline—they consistently exceed expectations.

> – Patric Young, Author of *Sit to Rise: Turning Your Darkest Pain into Your Brightest Victory*

The team at Streamline is amazing! The process of getting my book completed was very organized, and they had my best interest the entire way. The ROI on this first book is so great that I'm getting ready to start my second book!!

> – Travis Janko, Author of *You, of All People: Outrageous Stories & Billion-Dollar Lessons from a SaaS Sales VP Turned 7-Figure Recruiting*

I'm so grateful for the Streamline team whose expert guidance helped shape my manuscript into its final form. The team's insightful and unwavering commitment to excellence and authenticity elevated my book beyond what I ever thought possible. They didn't just help streamline the process for me as an author, they pulled the best out of me through the Streamline process.

> – Bryan Schwartz, Author of *Worthy Opponents: How God Uses Opposition, Enemies, and Adversity for Your Growth and Good*

Are there enough positive adjectives out there to describe Streamline?! And their team?! And ALL THE THINGS?! No! There are not! But if I had to pick a few: amazing, exceptional, intentional, relentless, passionate, and purposeful are a few that come to mind (are those adjectives? 😁). I truly can't say enough about Streamline and their team. If you want to work with PEOPLE that you know, like, and trust, I highly recommend them. They have this incredible way of making you feel comfortable and encouraging growth at the same time. I'm so thankful for them ALL, and they truly have servant hearts! 🙏LETS GOOOOOO!

> – Brittany Richmond, Author of *Lies My Anxiety Has Told Me: Going from "Suffering From" to "Living With" Anxiety*

THE **WORLD** NEEDS **YOUR BOOK**

THE WORLD NEEDS YOUR BOOK

Streamline the Process and Unlock Your Purpose

ALEX DEMCZAK   **WILL SEVERNS**

THE WORLD NEEDS YOUR BOOK
Streamline the Process and Unlock Your Purpose

Copyright © 2024 by Alex Demczak and Will Severns

All rights reserved. No part of this book may be reproduced, distributed, or transmitted in any form or by any means, including photocopying, recording, or other electronic or mechanical methods, without the written permission from the publisher or author, except as permitted by U.S. copyright law or in the case of brief quotations embodied in a book review.

Disclaimer: Although the publisher and the author have made every effort to ensure that the information in this book was correct at press time and while this publication is designed to provide accurate information in regard to the subject matter covered, the publisher and the author assume no responsibility for errors, inaccuracies, omissions, or any other inconsistencies herein and hereby disclaim any liability to any party for any loss, damage, or disruption caused by errors or omissions, whether such errors or omissions result from negligence, accident, or any other cause.

Interior Layout and Design: Stephanie Anderson
Editorial Team: Mandi Reed, Cindy McCachern
Cover Design: Abigael Elliott

ISBNs:
979-8-89165-194-4 *Paperback*
979-8-89165-195-1 *Hardback*
979-8-89165-196-8 *E-book*

Published by:
Streamline Books
Kansas City, MO
streamlinebookspublishing.com

 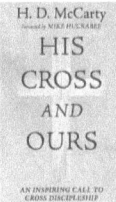  

writemybooks.com

CONTENTS

INTRODUCTION 1

THE BESTSELLER MINDSET

1 The Impact of One 9
2 Bestseller Redefined 15
3 The World Needs Your Book 21
4 Someone You Have Yet to Meet is Counting on You to Get Better Today 29
5 Stories Connect Us 35
6 From Generation to Generation 43
7 Hidden Impact 47

WRITE, EDIT, PUBLISH, REPEAT

8 With the End in Mind 55
9 Ideation 59
10 Outline 65
11 Writing 71

12	Don't Seek to Get Published; Seek to Get Edited	77
13	Cover Design	85
14	Interior Layout/Design	91
15	Proofreading	97
16	Book Launch	101
17	Printing	111
18	Community	119

THE STREAMLINE PROCESS

19	Differentiator #1: Our Turnkey Process	125
20	Differentiator #2: Our Human-Centered Team	133
21	Differentiator #3: Our Community	141
AFTERWORD		145

INTRODUCTION
Will and Alex

WHETHER YOU'VE ADMITTED it to your colleagues, friends, parents, spouse, or yourself, you're reading these words because, deep down, *you know there's a book burning inside of you.*

We started our business to help leaders like you bring their books to life because we believe the world needs your story and wisdom. Yes, we said it—the world needs *your* story and wisdom.

However, in our experience, we've seen many potential authors shy away from articulating their stories on paper. Why? They look at social media and see authors promoting books in large forums like morning news shows and national conferences. They read bestseller lists. Then, even though their message keeps lighting them up inside, imposter syndrome creeps in and shakes their confidence. *I'm not a celebrity or influencer. Who am I to write a book? Who am I to share this story?*

At the same time, major publishers confirm imposter syndrome by publishing fewer and fewer "undiscovered" authors. These publishers want guaranteed bestsellers, and they bank on celebrity and six- or seven-figure social media followings to rack up book sales.

From our perspective, a book is *more* than a sale—it's the story you were meant to share with the world. A book is also more than what we typically see at conferences. While we love conferences and they offer valuable opportunities, we've observed that they can be a double-edged sword.

For some authors, conferences present a wealth of opportunities, yet they can also reinforce imposter syndrome. Most conference speakers—from Mel Robbins to Tony Robbins—are well-known and have sold a ton of books. It is easy to let their success get in your way and overshadow your own aspirations. You might find yourself applauding their achievements while doubting your abilities, questioning who wants to hear what you say.

Focusing on the person standing on stage is easy when you are part of an audience. But try flipping your perspective and asking yourself: How much wisdom is *sitting* in that room? We all have people in our lives—perhaps an uncle or someone from our church—who possesses just as much wisdom as someone published by a major book publisher. However, they may not know how to capture that wisdom on paper. Often, they believe writing a bestseller is the only path to success.

Hey, bestsellers are great, and we want your book to be successful. But what if the pressure of writing a "bestseller" is holding you back from writing the book you're meant to write? What if you're destined to write something even *better* than a bestseller?

Bring a Team Around Your Dream

We believe in your book because we believe in you. It's as simple as that. We believe you have a story to share, the expertise to tell it, and the platform to make an impact. Your message is something the world desperately needs to hear.

We also believe the book burning inside you is there for a reason. God, in *His* infinite wisdom, entrusted you with that story, that message, because you're the right person for the job. We wholeheartedly believe at least one person needs to read the book in your head that won't go away. That's why it's there.

Free yourself from the expectation and burden of writing a bestseller. Instead, focus on writing the book you were meant to write. By doing so, you'll gain the freedom to walk forward confidently, putting your story on paper for someone—whether present or future—who is meant to benefit from your insight. By starting with one person in mind, we're confident your message will resonate and ripple out to reach all the places and people in the world it's meant to touch. Remember, you don't have to do it alone—do it with a supportive team around you.

Our team has identified ten key components necessary to write and publish a book independently: Ideation, Outline, Writing, Editing, Cover Design, Interior Layout, Proofreading, Book Launch, Printing, and Community.

This book will guide you through these ten components, empowering you to begin the writing and editing process today. By learning about these components, you will be empowered to leverage technological advancements, such as self-publishing, that have opened countless new avenues to publication, unlike anything in the history of books.

We've discovered creating a book alone is like being the lone gazelle separated from the herd. Sooner or later, doubt creeps in like a stalking lion, and you begin to question whether your message is worth sharing with the world. As Stephen Pressfield articulates in *The War of Art,* this resistance lies at the heart of your hesitation. It fuels the belief that the world *doesn't* need your book.

We have talked with countless authors who have expressed a desire to write a book for years, even decades. However, when we ask who has helped them in this endeavor, they often respond that no one has. They tried to pursue authorship alone and struggled to gain traction. While it's possible to write a book alone, it is no easy task. That's why assembling a team around your dream is so important.

Here's the thing: writing a book is a huge deal. It can be challenging when you're the only person carrying the weight of all your ideas, hopes, dreams, fears, intentions, and the work it takes to write, edit, proofread, design, and launch a book. But when you come alongside others to help you hold it aloft, it suddenly feels lighter. It's not only doable but also more fun and exciting.

We have a "Turnkey Publishing Process" designed to bring your book to life with the help of writers, editors, project managers, and designers who support you every step of the way. Most importantly, we offer a community and a proven process that energizes and excites us to come to work each day. We love collaborating with talented people to turn your ideas into reality. In other words, our secret sauce is building a fantastic community around you, and it all starts with you and your story.

One Last Thing

We want this book to help you understand *why* we believe the world needs your book. Parts One and Three delve into the why and what of book writing, editing, and publishing, while Part Two focuses on how to create your book.

Part One is dedicated to something we've grown passionate about: reframing author success. We believe authors who start with a renewed vision for success are the ones best positioned to share their stories with the world effectively.

Part Two details each step you must take to bring your book to life. Publishing has evolved to the point where you *can* fulfill this dream on your own. Although having support is highly beneficial, we know it's possible to write, edit, and publish your book with dedicated time, energy, and effort. With that being said…

Part Three will explore the process we've developed at Streamline to help individuals bring their books to life. This involves working with a team of experts through our "Turnkey Publishing Process." We have worked diligently on this process for years, and are proud of the team that helped us formulate and solidify each step. We now invite you to view the chapters ahead as a one-on-one conversation between you and us, the co-founders of Streamline.

We are fortunate to operate within a community of talented, people-first publishing companies with several exceptional options. We hope you choose to collaborate with one of them. It doesn't necessarily have to be us—although we would be delighted if it were! What matters most is that you have a supportive team by your side.

We're happy you're here with us now and eagerly anticipate sharing the upcoming pages with you. It's the book *we knew* couldn't stay inside us any longer. We've put in the effort, alongside our dedicated Streamline team, to ensure this book reaches your hands.

One day, you'll be able to say the same, and we genuinely can't wait to hold the book you were born to write. You have a book inside you; it doesn't need to stay inside for much longer.

Let's go!

– Will Severns and Alex Demczak

THE BESTSELLER MINDSET

CHAPTER 1

The Impact of One

ALEX

IT WAS A Thursday afternoon in the cornfields of Iowa, and I found myself driving to my third speaking engagement of the day, with one more still to go. You heard that correctly—four speaking engagements in just twelve hours! While speaking four times in the same day was exhilarating, it was also undeniably exhausting.

This crazy day became more manageable when I convinced my wife, Erin, to join me for one of the engagements—an elementary school assembly in Iowa. It was an incredible experience. Erin, a former first-grade teacher, effortlessly took to the stage. The kids adored her, making it clear she was the favorite, hands down!

After the assembly (my third talk of the day), Erin headed home while I prepared for my final engagement of the night—a community gathering for a local school in Iowa. As Erin left, I hit the hotel weight room for a workout and received a text from my friend, Daniel Decker.

Daniel played a crucial role in launching the book I co-wrote with my mentor, Jon Gordon, titled *The Sale,* a business fable about integrity. With a stellar reputation in the publishing industry, Daniel has assisted leaders like Tony Robbins, Roma Downey, Lewis Howes, Pat Flynn, and many others in launching their books. His message read, "Don't tell anyone this yet. But tomorrow, it will be announced that your book will hit the *Wall Street Journal Bestsellers List."*

I was in disbelief. An instant rush of excitement ran through my body. While this would be a significant first for me, it was yet another accomplishment for my co-author, Jon Gordon, who has produced not just one bestseller but many. In other words, I finally tasted what my mentor had experienced multiple times. Jon's best-selling book, *The Energy Bus,* has sold millions of copies, and many of his books are utilized by successful companies, professional sports teams, and school districts.

You've likely heard books classified as *New York Times, USA Today,* or *Wall Street Journal* bestsellers. In short, landing on one of these bestseller lists requires selling a certain number of books during the first week of your book launch. (The rules differ for Amazon bestseller lists, which we will cover in Chapter 2.) Many such lists are somewhat subjective, and there have been some notorious instances of people attempting to game the system to appear on these well-known lists. Some of these stories have resulted in lawsuits or caused people to question an author's character. Did they want to write a meaningful book or just be seen as someone who cracked the bestseller code?

Knowing many people had bought and read the book Jon and I wrote together was an honor. As I worked out in the weight room that day, I felt great. I was about to crush some weights and would soon crush my final speaking engagement of the day.

The event was organized by a small school district in Iowa, about five hours from my hometown of Columbia, Missouri. They had invited community members, parents, and students to hear my talk that night. I remember it was scheduled for Thursday at 7 p.m. Although I was a bit bummed about missing Thursday Night Football, I was excited to give one final speech at the end of a good day. Then I had a cool thought...

This group of students and teachers are in for a treat. They get to hear from one of the newest bestselling authors in America.

With confidence, I got into my car and headed toward the school. However, when I arrived, something felt off. The parking lot was empty. My first thought was that a bus would soon arrive, bringing the crowd. I got out of my car and entered the building, wondering if everyone was already inside. As I walked toward the room where I was scheduled to speak, I couldn't believe what I saw...

One kid.

One fourth-grade kid was sitting in the bleachers!

I looked down at my watch. It was 7 o'clock, the scheduled start of the speaking engagement. Frustration hit me instantly. I had nothing against Iowa, but this small town was not where

I wanted to be. I thought about being away from my family, exhausted from all the speaking engagements that day, and how I could have been watching Thursday Night Football instead of speaking at a random school with only one kid in attendance.

At the time, I was on a nationwide book tour, traveling to companies, schools, and teams to share the message of *The Sale*. In many ways, this book tour was about me and how I could share *my* message. I was humbled and taken aback. I started to sweat from a mix of anger or embarrassment—probably a bit of both. How could it be that on the same day I landed on the *Wall Street Journal* Bestsellers List, only *one* kid showed up for my talk?!

As I walked toward the fourth grader to introduce myself, a thought suddenly gave me chills.

Who am I to overlook this ONE person?

In an instant, I was humbled by my prideful feelings. Since when was I above talking with a child? When did my success and excitement become solely dependent on the number of attendees at my talks?

As I approached the boy, I recognized him from the school assembly earlier that day. He had been one of the more positive and energetic students, especially when my wife was getting the crowd on their feet and cheering. I spent a few minutes encouraging his positivity. When his dad joined us a few minutes later, I thanked them for coming and gave them free signed copies of my book. I guess fourth graders can read business books too. You gotta get them started young!

That fourth-grader was the reason I was in Iowa. I didn't find a packed house with two hundred people, but I found one person I couldn't overlook. As I walked out of the gym, the humiliation and embarrassment I had when I first arrived was gone. I recognized I was exactly where I was meant to be. Another win from the night was that, instead of giving my fourth talk, the three school administrators took me out to eat at Buffalo Wild Wings. That night was a victory for all of us!

CHAPTER 2

Bestseller Redefined

ALEX

LET'S ACKNOWLEDGE SOMETHING right away: the dream of writing a bestseller is *incredibly* compelling. Why wouldn't it be? The world tells us that appearing on a bestseller list, such as those from *Publisher's Weekly* and *The New York Times*, inevitably leads to acclaim, fame, and book sales that could make you, like J.K. Rowling, richer than the Queen. And yes, a spot on the *New York Times* Bestseller List *can* lead to all those things. Just ask James Patterson, who has appeared on the *New York Times* Bestseller List more than any other author in history. The red carpet has been very real for him. But as you saw from my story in Chapter 1, it doesn't always go that way.

The bestseller dream can die hard. It is so complex that many authors, as mentioned previously, try to game the system

[REDEFINE]
BESTSELLER

to appear on the lists. Now, let that soak in for a minute. Why would authors try to game the system? It's simple–*because there's a system to be gamed.*

Your Princess is in Another Castle

Getting your book on a prestigious, official bestseller list usually requires selling around five thousand or more copies in a single week. The rules seem straightforward, but they are more complex than they appear.

In 1986, the book world learned how cloak-and-dagger a bestseller list can be. In a widely documented court case, William Peter Blatty, author of *The Exorcist*, sued the *New York Times* for leaving his book, *Legion*, off its famed bestseller list. The Times responded that its bestseller list was not objective but *editorial*. The lower courts agreed with them, and the Supreme Court refused to hear an appeal. Translation: The *New York Times* Bestseller list can be *whatever they want*. More recently, in 2023, James Patterson accused the *Times* of "cooking the books" that appear on their bestseller list to reflect the titles and authors they prefer.

Additionally, other factors complicate which authors make the list. One of those factors is which list you're hoping to appear on. In most cases, authors who hit the Amazon Bestseller list sold a certain number of books in their category within a few hours. Sounds even more daunting. But consider this: Sometimes, those authors *did* sell a lot of books. Others didn't, yet they still got the "bestseller" designation because they understood the actual game: *niche categorization*. Categorize your book in a small enough niche, and it won't take many sales to reach "bestseller" status in that category.

So, while counting sales is notoriously difficult, not every list-maker is looking at the same numbers. According to *Lit Hub*, the *New York Times* is notorious for keeping its cards close to the chest. It rarely discloses how it tracks sales (or which retailers it favors).

And all the hush-hush and "editorializing" have inadvertently created the system many authors now try to game. Think of it this way: if appearing on a bestseller list is Princess Peach and you're Mario, dodging every mushroom and winged duck on your book journey, your Princess will almost always be in another castle.

Die to the List

Despite it all, publishers typically lean into the bestseller myth. They may not outright promise their authors they'll write a bestseller. Still, their marketing, mission statements, and splashy online presence are carefully crafted to reinforce the idea that writing a bestseller is *the* ultimate success, and they are the publisher to help an author achieve it. When an author's book doesn't rise to that level of success, all their efforts and resources seem wasted, and the publisher often blames them for their lack of sales.

Sound frustrating? We agree. That's why we believe every aspiring author should move beyond the obsession with *bestseller lists*.

We are not saying you shouldn't aim for success. However, we want you to recognize the bestseller list for the smokescreen it is. Wave away the smoke and see the life-changing truth: your success as an author is *much more* than seeing your name and title on someone else's arbitrary list.

Most importantly, we want to redefine success so the book you're meant to write reaches the hearts and minds of those who need your message. For us, that's what it means to "die to the list": trading the *fantasy* of impact for something *real*. A list doesn't make someone's life better, but your book will. *That* is our definition of success.

The Chick-fil-A of Book Publishing

We'd love Streamline to be seen as the Chick-fil-A of book publishing. Chick-fil-A stands out in the fast-food industry by prioritizing quality over profit. They prioritize quality food, service, and a memorable overall experience, distinguishing themselves from the typical industry emphasis on maximizing profits at any cost.

In other words, if there's a "bestseller list" for chicken and fries, Chick-fil-A abandoned it long ago. *Quality*—not profit—is their definition of success. If you've ever driven past a Chick-fil-A and seen the seemingly endless drive-thru lines snaking around the building, through the parking lot, and even out onto the roads leading to the restaurant, you know the result. By reframing what success means to their organization, Chick-fil-A positively impacts millions of people *every single day*.

Streamline shares that vision for positive impact. That's why we've reframed our success as a company and organization to focus on bringing your book to the world.

To get there, we need you to recognize how important and impactful the book inside you will be. We're thrilled you picked up this book so we can invite you to step courageously into the vision with us and die to the list every day.

This approach empowers us to walk away from the expectations, false hopes, and foundationless ideas about what "writing a bestseller" can do for us and focus on how your book can change the world for someone else.

We can't wait for you to do the same—and to see where that boldness takes you.

CHAPTER 3

The World Needs Your Book

WILL

> "Does the world need my story?"
> "Who would even read it?"

DO THESE QUESTIONS feel familiar? We hear them often. It's unfortunate but not surprising, given how many publishers boast about the number of authors they turn away or books they reject due to doubts about their commercial appeal. This perpetuates the notion that only *certain* stories are worth telling. Other companies imply your book will likely end up in *Oprah's Book Club* or be championed on podcasts everywhere. Both approaches reinforce the bestseller myth and feed imposter syndrome, leading potential authors to believe they have nothing worthwhile to share.

When we established Streamline, we aimed to break this mold. Those grandiose claims and promises made by other publishers don't sit well with us. They've only fueled the doubts and resistance that prevent authors from getting their stories on paper. As mentioned earlier, Stephen Pressfield highlights in *The War of Art* how Resistance (with a capital "R") can be so formidable it paralyzes us. In other words, Resistance will go to great lengths to prevent us from doing the creative work we were born to undertake.

Much of that Resistance stems from impostor syndrome. We convince ourselves we don't have the time or resources to pursue our goals. However, even when we overcome that lie, the world quickly supplies plenty of other excuses to take its place. *"I don't have the time," "I don't have the resources,"* and *"No one will read my book"* are all lies the world tells us to keep us from writing a book.

But it isn't easy to make an impact when we allow these thoughts to dictate our actions. Writing for "the world" can feel as daunting as writing a "bestseller"—a huge mental hurdle. However, once you overcome this obstacle, you can move forward with courage again.

That's why we're here.

The Heart of This Book

We wrote this book to provide specific strategies for sharing your story with the world. We aim to empower you to make your message available to those who most need it. While there are countless platforms for publishing your message, we firmly believe a book surpasses any tweet, blog, or blurb. A book presents your message in its fully realized form and makes it portable. It can cross state lines, ideological boundaries, and even centuries, enduringly impacting readers.

We're confident *the world needs more stories.* So, we want to encourage you to share the light of your story from your perspective and unique expertise. This is vital in a world filled with noisy news updates, depressing conflicts, and mindless, addictive "feeds."

In the early 2000's, it was noted that eighty-one percent of people today want to write a book, yet only one percent do so each year. That statistic is staggering to us. It suggests most people have a deep-seated desire to share their story through a book but are hindered by life's challenges. They have been so beaten down by the world, exhausted, overworked, and overlooked that they never get around to doing it. Our Streamline mission is to bridge that gap. We strive to help more people accomplish their goal of writing and publishing a great book of which they can be proud. (We sometimes pinch ourselves in disbelief that we get to play a small role in making this happen.)

If you're part of the eighty-one percent, we celebrate that you've picked up this book. Keep reading. Allow us to guide you toward becoming part of the one percent who have accomplished this remarkable feat. Our goal is to help you create a resource and leave a legacy in book form that will resonate with future generations—an impact beginning with one.

Writing for a World of One

We've heard it suggested that when someone claims they only want to impact one person, they are hiding behind their fear of failure. Many people grapple with that idea. Critics often say it's easy for an author to make such claims when they have sold millions of books and earned tens of thousands for a single speaking engagement. To say you only want to reach one person can be a way to protect yourself from feeling let down if your book doesn't sell a million copies.

You probably know the drill: undersell your expectations upfront, and then, when someone asks you how the book is doing later, you can talk openly about it. Managing expectations from the beginning is a great strategy that can set you up for impactful success. However, our message differs from that statement by recognizing the absolute *necessity* of the person who needs your book.

When a potential author says, "If only one person benefits from my book, it's worth it," our ears perk up. We think, *"Wow, here's someone ready for the book-writing journey."* What sets this kind of author apart from someone aiming to sell a million copies? Simply put, they have the right mindset.

We stand by our core belief: The world needs your book. However, we define "the world" as something closer to home. Whether it's your business, nonprofit, ministry, or family, a world closer to home needs what you have to offer.

Think of it this way: The New Testament is filled with stories of Jesus spending time with individuals—the woman who touched his cloak, the tax collector, the blind man, the rich man, and many others. Some might see those as small stories with minor impacts. Yet, here we are, reading and learning from them two thousand years later. Jesus never lost sight of ministering and preaching to the multitudes, but he focused much of his earthly ministry on the *one*.

Here's the bottom line: You don't have to be a celebrity. You have a book to offer because *you* have a story. To date, we've had the privilege of working with over a hundred authors. We believe that is a massive accomplishment. But we've hardly begun to uncover the hundreds, thousands, and even millions of stories needing to be told—including yours.

ALEX

Reflecting on Iowa

That Thursday night in Iowa changed me. Now, whenever I travel, speak, or write books, my goal is no longer to reach the masses. Instead, I focus on impacting the one person who could be encouraged by my message.

Don't get me wrong; it was an unbelievable honor for the book I co-wrote with Jon Gordon to be featured on a bestseller list. We were mentioned alongside prolific authors like Adam Grant, Jocko Willink, James Clear, and many other notable names. I will forever be grateful to Jon Gordon, one of the top leadership authors and speakers in America, for taking a chance and teaming with me to write *The Sale*. It was a mountaintop moment to write and publish our book together. However, I learned that hitting a list shouldn't be the main goal for any author.

I assumed hitting a bestseller list would change my life. As humbling and honoring as it was, it didn't. Our book was featured on the list, but the next week, it was replaced by other bestsellers. Hitting a bestseller list, having a certain number of social media followers, or making a certain amount of money is not what life is all about. While these achievements can be positive, they ultimately leave you unfulfilled if they are all you pursue or bank on.

After Tom Brady won his fourth Super Bowl ring while married to a professional model and admired by millions, he said, "There has to be more to life than this." Similarly, Jim Carrey once said, "I wish everyone could be rich and famous so they could experience it for themselves and understand that it is not all it is cracked up to be."

There are more lasting and valuable reasons to share your story with the world. We wrote this book to remind you that the message burning inside you is the encouragement someone else desperately needs. It may not be for millions, thousands, or even hundreds, but perhaps it's exactly what one person needs to hear. Our culture teaches us that our worth is defined by the number of "likes" we receive on social media or the quantity of books we sell, convincing us that these metrics determine whether we are a "somebody." This couldn't be further from the truth.

God created each of us uniquely, providing us with gifts and skills to utilize for God's glory and the good of others. When you finally decide to share your message with the world, you might find yourself on a Thursday night in Iowa like I did. When you walk into that room, I hope you can put your ego aside and focus on the ONE person who needs your message.

Focus on making an impact, one person at a time. As you set out to write your book, start by asking, *"Who is the one person who needs this message?"* You will be amazed at the book you can write when you ask that question.

CHAPTER 4

Someone You Have Yet to Meet is Counting on You to Get Better Today

---

ALEX

The Power of Mentorship

A S A COLLEGE athlete at the University of Missouri, I often listened to excellent speakers who visited campus. The most notable one was bestselling author and speaker Jon Gordon. Before I heard Jon speak, one of my teammates, Michael Godas, gave me a copy of Jon's bestselling book, *The Energy Bus*. Drawn to the book's message—how positivity can create personal and professional success—I devoured it in a few short days.

I was amazed when Jon visited campus and spoke to the athletic department. He had a unique ability to captivate college athletes who had spent their day listening to professors and coaches. Inspired by his talk, I made it a point to connect with Jon afterward. I told him how much I loved his message and asked if I could learn to do what he did as an author and speaker.

"Would you be willing to volunteer your time and work for me in exchange?" he asked.

I immediately agreed. The rest is history. Jon has mentored me for eight years at the time of this writing. He even mentioned our mentoring relationship during a National Speakers Association keynote of twelve hundred influential speaking professionals. This shoutout was a byproduct of those years of mentorship, earning his trust and adding value to his work. Learning from one of America's best authors and keynote speakers for nearly a decade has been invaluable. Jon continues to be generous with advice and support in my career. Our mentorship also led to us writing *The Sale* together.

I share this example of mentorship in my life for two reasons. First, it would never have happened if I hadn't stepped out of my comfort zone and asked. Second, I want you to realize that someone in your life right now might be willing to mentor you if you ask them. Gleaning wisdom from a mentor can catapult your career forward by years. Today, as an author and speaker, I travel the country, sharing messages to encourage people to become the best versions of themselves and succeed at work and home. As a result, I pursued this work full-time much more quickly because my mentor challenged and encouraged me.

What You Decide Today

Much of what has happened in my career in the last eight years—the speaking engagements, co-authoring *The Sale*, and even founding Streamline—would not have been possible without Jon's dedication to continuous improvement. Jon's story is rooted in the grind of working hard to succeed, and he has experienced incredible wins. However, if he had decided to stop pushing and keep moving forward at any point in his career, our paths might never have crossed. During those early days of relentless effort, he had no idea how much I was counting on him to keep going—and neither did I. But that doesn't change the fact that *I was*.

Significantly, you're holding this book. You are the person we've been addressing all along—the one with a story burning inside. We hope that by reading this, you'll find the courage to move forward and write it. Will and I love the line that "Someone you have yet to meet is counting on you to get better today." Someone in your future will depend on you to take action. What you choose to do from this moment on—whether you act or not—will potentially change the course of your life. Think of it this way: what if we had decided *not* to write the book that was burning inside us?

One Book Can Change It All

After traveling to Nashville for a speaking engagement, I had the chance to visit the headquarters of Ramsey Solutions— the company Dave Ramsey founded and has grown into a very successful financial coaching business. With over a thousand employees and three hundred million dollars in annual revenue, Ramsey Solutions is renowned for its thriving work environment and exceptional company culture. People who work there consistently rave about how great the company culture is, even with its steady growth. Ramsey Solutions helps individuals manage their money well through the fantastic resources they have developed.

While at Ramsey Solutions, I had the privilege of meeting Dave Ramsey and thanking him for being a mentor figure to me from afar, just as he has been for thousands of others. After meeting Dave, I received a tour of the facility from my excellent tour guide, Margaret Kloss, who showed me a wall displaying Ramsey Solutions' history. Seeing the timeline of the organization's accomplishments was inspiring, but the best part of the tour was seeing where it all started.

During the tour, I snapped a picture of the company's timeline because one thing stood out to me: the origin story. This incredible company began with Dave writing and self-publishing his first book in 1992.

Amazingly, a book was the first milestone on this impressive timeline. While the rest of the wall highlights the company's other outstanding accomplishments, I marveled at that initial milestone– Ramsey Solutions started with a book. Dave

Ramsey wrote one book because he believed in his message and expertise, and it changed everything.

But that's just Dave's story. Even if your personal and professional journey doesn't lead to a multi-million-dollar company with hundreds or thousands of employees, it's still worth asking the question: What will your book have the power to change?

CHAPTER 5

Stories Connect Us

WILL

ALEX HAD BEEN telling me for six months to watch *The Chosen*. Despite its growing popularity and evident impact, my wife, Lauren, and I hadn't found the time to dive into it. When we finally did, I was pleasantly surprised—as faith-based film and media haven't consistently been critically acclaimed. But regardless of any accolades from Academy Awards (which is a bit like the film version of landing on a bestseller list), the creators of *The Chosen* had something far more significant in mind.

In the first episode of the second season, Jesus engages in a conversation with a man who had committed a heinous act: he had beaten another man, stolen his horse, and ended up breaking his leg in the process. Without giving away any spoilers, it's safe to say that by the time this man encounters Jesus, he is consumed by shame over his actions. He hesitates to reveal their full extent, fearing judgment from Jesus.

But Jesus responds compassionately, assuring the man, "I want to hear your story. Stories connect us." This moment highlights the profound power of being heard and understood by others, even when acknowledging our past mistakes and vulnerabilities. Through this scene, Jesus emphasizes that sharing our stories with honesty and vulnerability often fosters deep connections with others.

Less News, More Stories

At Streamline, we often highlight our pursuit of "Less news and more stories." This brief phrase encapsulates our mission over the past few years and our commitment to moving forward. Simply put, we aim for a world with fewer headlines and ever-changing social media feeds, and more space for long-form storytelling.

Achieving this goal is no small feat, especially in today's cultural climate. News cycles continue unabated, showing little sign of slowing down anytime soon. It often feels like we are inundated with a relentless stream of news, social media updates, and content designed for quick consumption. In this fast-paced environment, where ideas are conceived, captured, and posted in about thirty seconds, why invest the hours and effort required to put a story down on paper?

For us, the answer lies in simple math. Stories told through enduring mediums create unique connections that even excellent, well-written, and researched news articles never can. Reading a brief article or headline about someone only scratches the surface of who they truly are. Short-form writing, by its nature, can only convey a limited amount of information, leaving readers prone to making assumptions about the subject or writer. This is especially true when they've been "canceled" or said something that clashes with their reader's values and beliefs. This is fertile ground for building walls, not connections.

On the other hand, taking the time to get your story down on paper helps others understand where you're coming from. It provides context to your beliefs, experiences, and the wisdom you've gained along the way. Then, instead of being dismissed for one social media post, you cultivate a connection with the people you want to reach the most.

That's not what you get by posting blurbs on social media, but we believe it's the understanding we need today. After all, isn't this why Jesus was invested in hearing the thief's story? He recognized the universality of feelings like shame and regret, offering compassion and support to those in need, regardless of their past actions. Despite all that, or maybe *because* of it, Jesus responded, "I care about you and how your heart is *today*. I care about how I can help you."

ALEX

Like many, I grew up as a sports fanatic. My grandpa always told me, "Alex, I was so dedicated to football when I was young that I didn't even date girls during football season." Although I went on a few dates, I was dedicated just like him. Fast-forward to college, and I had the opportunity to walk on the football team at the University of Missouri.

As a football player at a major university, life was fantastic. Everything was falling into place, and I was in the zone. I felt unstoppable. However, this feeling changed when I entered my junior year and Mizzou transitioned from The Big 12 to the Southeastern Conference (SEC).

The season began with the usual meeting with one of my assistant coaches. Full of breezy confidence, I entered the room to find three coaches seated at the table where there had before been one. This was different since the meeting had been a low-key pat on the back for the past two seasons. I optimistically expected this year to follow suit and to be the year I would start moving up. But this time, when I entered the room and took my seat, one of the coaches stood up to close the door behind me. This was not a good start.

"Alex, I want to shoot you straight," one of the coaches began. He looked squarely at me across the table. "We're over-scholarshipped at quarterback. We're bringing in someone to take your spot."

At the time, football was my everything—my life, my identity, all of it. As the saying goes, the jersey defined me. This coach was telling me I wasn't good enough to wear it. I didn't measure up.

"You have two options," he continued. "Option one, you're cut. Option two, you get to stay on as a volunteer assistant coach. We could use you around here. But you need to decide right now, in this meeting."

My mind raced as I tried to process what was happening. What would *staying on as coach* even look like? Still now, I feel a tug in my spirit.

"I'll stay on as a coach," I said.

The coaches stood up, shook my hand, and escorted me out of the room. I walked past the new quarterback—the guy chosen to replace me. It was tough.

I walked out to my truck feeling humiliated and lost. I climbed into the cab, let go, and wept. There I was, a kid from a small town with all these dreams—and I'd just arrived at the end of my story. I felt like I'd let so many people down, including myself.

But I rallied for the first day of practice. I thought of Nick Saban, who'd made a fortune going the coaching route. Maybe I could eventually follow in his footsteps. I thought I would step into an influential role as an assistant coach. Maybe I would even get put into the press box to call the occasional play.

"Alex," one of the coaches barked at me the first morning. He handed me a yellow referee flag. "We need you to bring this flag to practice. When someone jumps offside, take the flag and throw it down."

"Oh," I responded.

I was instructed to take this small yellow flag and drop it… and that was it. The worst part was he showed me how to do it. Twice.

"What part of practice?" I asked.

"The entire season," he said. "This is your role."

In other words, I'd immediately gone from being an SEC Quarterback to a professional flag thrower. And "professional flag-thrower" isn't even an actual title.

As you can imagine, it was a tough season. I spent my junior year making coffee for the coaches, printing off copies of the practice plan, and attending practice in my street clothes. I grew frustrated, even angry. My thoughts ran in a continuous loop: *God, you gave me this passion for football. You gave me the ability to do it. Why did you allow this to happen?*

I resolved to do everything I could to return to the team my senior year. So, I ran sprints after practice with the quarterbacks (yes, in my street clothes). I stuck with my weight training and did everything else I could think of. My dedication was so evident that other players began to ask why I bothered—even as they acknowledged how great it was that I could keep up.

As I continued to stick with it and try to add value to those around me, players and coaches began to take note of my commitment to the program. During that time, I received many encouraging words from people who saw me staying dedicated every day. Those small encouragements helped me persevere, teaching me the humility that comes from being brought so low. During those challenging moments, I also began to form relationships that remain incredibly influential in my life. Eventually, I came full circle with the team. I rejoined my senior year as a quarterback. We went to the Citrus Bowl and beat the Minnesota Gophers, and my senior season was a fantastic experience.

Looking back, I can see that before I could experience the joy of my senior year, I had to learn a difficult but critical lesson: you don't need a specific job or position to show up every day and be excellent at everything you do.

Leadership doesn't require a title. I made a much more significant impact the year I threw that flag than in all my years as a player. If I hadn't had that year, I wouldn't be speaking and writing books today. If I hadn't had the experience of being brought so low that I had to depend on God, even while I questioned why he would allow something like that to happen to me, I wouldn't have this story to write or tell.

Today, I tell this story every time I speak. Each time I do, the room becomes so quiet you can hear a pin drop. It has taught me that people listen when we're vulnerable and honest about our experiences. This is where genuine connection happens.

The shame I felt in the coach's office is similar to that of the horse thief in *The Chosen*. While that's a two-thousand-year-old example, we face modern versions of it every day. Let's be honest—whether it happened in the principal's office or after being fired from a job, we've all had moments of shame and humiliation. We all have stories to tell about those times. It is incredibly powerful when we share them, and our pin-drop moment is met by someone who wants to listen to and connect with us on a deeper level.

Seeing the humiliation I once felt come full circle is incredibly powerful. Now, I confidently encourage individuals at all levels of their company to be leaders. I can assure every person they can show up and be excellent without a fancy title or corner office because *I know it's true*. I've lived it. Whenever I share my story, there's an opportunity for someone else to see they, too, can be the best version of themselves, no matter where they are or what they're doing. As they become that person, their actions will ripple into future generations.

CHAPTER 6

From Generation to Generation

WILL

MY DAD, BILL SEVERNS, became an author when I was in high school, and it was the first time I'd seen someone in my immediate circle pursue authorship. Dad's book, *Keepers of the Sandlot*, was published in 2009 and invites parents and coaches of youth sports to consider the tough odds of a kid going on to play professional sports. It emphasizes that children only have a short time to play any game before they grow up. The book encourages parents and coaches to shift their priorities to ensure kids thoroughly enjoy their time playing rather than feeling pressured to become the next Olympic athlete. Dad's message underscores the tremendous influence parents and coaches have on kids' lives.

While *Keepers of the Sandlot* may not have achieved bestseller status, its profound impact on kids, families, and coaches is undeniable. That book has become a lasting part of my dad's legacy. Christian philanthropist Bill High shared an insight with Dad that changed his perspective. "Bill," he said, "you will never know the exact number of people you'll impact with your book on this side of heaven."

The wonderful thing is that quantifying impact is not our job. This wisdom, often shared with our Streamline authors, draws from 1 Corinthians 3, reminding us that our role is to plant seeds. Whether through our books, relationships, or other aspects of life, we are mere sowers, scattering seeds across the land. It's God who nurtures and makes the seeds grow. Our task is to trust him to bring the results.

The World Will Tell You Otherwise

ALEX

The world continually tries to define success for you, whether through the hundreds of marketing messages encountered daily or the hours spent glued to screens. It's all too easy to be influenced by the mixed messages from social media and mainstream media about what truly matters. Our team advocates for a shift in perspective on success, which begins with aligning your mindset, expectations, and goals with your values—not those imposed by society.

When you reach the end of your life and look back on your accomplishments, it won't be the money you made, or the bestseller lists you hit that stands out. Instead, you'll reflect on the impact you've had on the lives of others.

A recent study asked a poignant question to fifty people over the age of ninety-five: "If you could live your life again, what would you do differently?" The responses revealed three recurring themes:

1. Many expressed a desire to reflect more if allowed to live their lives again.
2. There was a common sentiment among respondents wishing they had taken more risks throughout their lives.
3. Many wanted to pursue activities that would leave a legacy beyond their lifetimes.

The third one hits home. These individuals overwhelmingly wanted to pursue endeavors that would last long after their passing. It's a stark reminder that someday, we will all die. Psalm 90:12 speaks to this saying, "Teach us to number our days so that we may gain a heart of wisdom."

What stands out from the study is that the nonagenarians didn't regret their lack of money, fame, or house size. Instead, they wished they had taken more time to reflect, risk, and make an impact. Their answers speak volumes about how we should spend our time. Instead of being caught up in insignificant details, we should follow the advice of these wise old folks and start living intentionally today!

Faithfulness = Impact

WILL

Respected authors such as Arthur Brooks and Tim Elmore often discuss two distinct life stages: fluid intelligence and crystallized intelligence. Fluid intelligence is a period of exploration during which individuals discover their preferences and gain new skills. According to this idea, holding onto fluid intelligence for too long can lead to a "midlife crisis." Instead, he advocates moving into crystallized intelligence, where accumulated wisdom and experiences are shared with the next generation.

I've watched my dad embody this principle over the years. He has faithfully delivered God's message, which has changed lives, including mine. Growing up, I saw the impact of Dad's book on others, and now, I find myself as a second-generation author.

Here you are, entrusted with a message God has given Alex and me to share with the world. What successes will sprout from the seeds you sow? What hidden impacts will your future book leave behind?

CHAPTER 7

Hidden Impact

WILL

A TERM WE'VE COINED is *"hidden impact"* to encapsulate the countless unforeseen outcomes that can occur when you write, launch, and publish your book, releasing it into the world. This concept is one of the key distinguishing factors of our company. While some might promise you the moon, we emphasize the more important reasons to share your message with the world.

What does hidden impact look like in real life? Many times, it manifests unexpectedly. It may be an email from a stranger thanking you for how your words transformed their life. It could manifest as a company or group buying multiple copies of your book, believing it will help their culture thrive. It might even be a person fifty years from now, halfway around the world, altering their life's course after finding your book on their parents' bookshelf and being moved by its message. As we've said before, there is no way to know the ripple effects of your message. But the hidden impact only happens—is only possible—if you write, edit, and publish your book.

Why We Beat a Dead Horse

Hopefully, by this point in the book, you'll know we're passionate about *reframing author success.* We want to revolutionize the publishing industry—that's the driving force behind our daily work. That's why we dedicated seven chapters to discuss the true essence of our mission and vision as both business owners and authors.

Throughout our journey, our team has had countless conversations with past, present, and future authors who share similarities with you, yet each carries a unique story. When we encourage them by saying the world needs their book, we often receive quizzical looks in response. We understand their uncertainty. That's when we introduce them to a different perspective—a world closer to home, where they can uncover the hidden impact awaiting them on the other side of their authorship journey.

If any part of you thought the first part of our book was repetitive or felt like it was "beating a dead horse," that is a good thing. Repetition can be a powerful tool in writing, and we believe this message is not only worth repeating but also *necessary* because of how conditioned we are to think about pursuing authorship.

Before co-founding Streamline with Alex, I was in a similar position. I had written a manuscript or two but was still figuring out what to do next. Should I submit them to a traditional publisher? Should I ask for feedback from friends? Or should I scrap my dream altogether and keep my writing to myself?

If you've asked these questions or wrestled with self-doubt, we hope you find value in the next part of the book, which focuses on taking action. Remember, you might need to reconsider if your goal is to make an impact as quickly as possible—whether in the next few months or years. The hidden impact of your book might stretch further out on a timeline than you may have anticipated. That's the reality that all begins with an idea between your ears.

Ten Key Components

From the moment you conceive an idea for a book, it's like the formation of a rain cloud gathering moisture. Slowly, your idea turns into thousands of thoughts about the book's potential. These thoughts are like raindrops falling from the sky and landing on one of two surfaces: water or land.

When raindrops hit land, the hope is for fertile growth. Good rain can foster the blossoming of flowers, the cultivation of crops, and the flourishing of trees. But in our full mountain stream graphic, designed by the talented Abigael

Elliott (who also designed our cover) you'll notice a series of raindrops cascading from the mountaintop and converging into a stream with purpose—contributing to something greater than themselves. Thus, we present a significant visual representation of the ten key components of writing, editing, and publishing a book.

THE 10-STEP BOOK PROCESS

1 - IDEATION
2 - OUTLINE
3 - WRITING
4 - EDITING
5 - COVER DESIGN
6 - INTERIOR LAYOUT
7 - PROOFREADING
8 - BOOK LAUNCH
9 - PRINTING
10 - COMMUNITY

WRITE, EDIT, PUBLISH, REPEAT

CHAPTER 8

With the End in Mind

WE LOVE THE image of the mountain stream for many reasons. It represents the *opposite* of an "uphill battle" that many associate with the book writing process. In other words, some might consider writing a book as climbing a mountain or venturing through a dark forest. Still, the mountain stream differs from those analogies. The journey should be fun, enjoyable, and flow freely when writing a book alongside a talented and professional team. That doesn't mean there won't be some scary moments along the way. Who hasn't encountered a few rapids? But even then, we have instructors to keep you at ease.

The mountain stream image encompasses ten key components of the book-writing process we've identified. We will explore each of those items in the coming chapters. We want to give you all the details—good, bad, and ugly—so you can decide whether to venture out into the book-writing process alone or if you want our talented team to help you bring your book to life. Whichever route you choose, we are confident we are giving you a crash course on effectively writing, editing, and publishing a book.

Know Your Audience Inside and Out

Identifying your audience is one of the critical first steps. Keep the person or group you are writing to in mind as you get your ideas and words on paper, letting the audience's needs, questions, and goals guide your words. The more specifically you can describe who you are writing to before you begin, the more likely your book will find them.

One way to do this is to think of someone in your life with a problem—sometimes called a pain point—that your book will address, alleviate, or even solve. Perhaps that person was the inspiration for your story. It can be beneficial to write a paragraph describing that person and reference it while writing. What does that person like and dislike? What do they want out of their personal or professional life? What stage of learning, earning, or parenting are they in? What burning questions do they have? What wisdom do they need to move forward?

Identify as many specifics about your audience as possible to establish guardrails that will hone your writing. If no single person comes to mind, think of a specific group. For example, "college seniors" may be too general to help guide your content but "college seniors saving for their first home purchase" is immediately clarifying.

Actions and Long-Term Goals

Professional writers and editors identify a distinct audience for every piece of writing they create. Then, they ask what action their reader should take after reading this book. For those college seniors, perhaps it's to develop and follow a budget. Working backward informs how your writing will come together and helps define the long-term goals for your book.

When it comes to these goals, separate them into two categories. The first category is how your book will help and encourage the reader to take a specific action and connect them with their purpose. The second category is about you and your personal goals for the book. Successfully meeting the goals for the reader will help you meet your personal goals.

One Streamline author, Randy Childress, did just that. Randy is a top financial advisor at a major financial firm. When Streamline published his book *Seasons of Selling*, Randy identified his goal as educating business owners and CPAs about successfully selling a business. He identified his personal goal as growing his own business by connecting readers to their purpose, naturally leading them to become his clients.

A Note on Goals

Books are as unique as the people who write them. We've seen firsthand how each person we work with has unique goals. Like Randy, some of our authors hope to educate their audience and grow their brand and business. Others are much more interested in preserving stories for their family.

Ultimately, your goals should be *your* goals. Identify your purpose and let go of the urge to compare your actions with others. Instead of looking around at other people, figure out how you will leverage your impact with this book. Once established, you can delve more deeply into the ten specific steps to breathe life into your book.

CHAPTER 9

Ideation

EVERY BOOK STARTS with a spark of inspiration. In the image of the mountain stream, the sun represents this initial ideation phase. It's a fitting representation, echoing the age-old wisdom, "There is nothing new under the sun." Indeed, our ideas often spring from the collective knowledge and experiences we've absorbed from others. As rain clouds converge and gather over the mountain, our thoughts and aspirations coalesce into a tangible vision for our book. If you sense a cloud forming in your mind, brimming with thoughts, words, and dreams of what your book could become, rain is in the forecast. When they fall, those drops will shape and nourish your manuscript until it is complete.

It's common for authors to feel pressured to develop a groundbreaking invention or concept for their book, fearing anything less wouldn't be "good enough." Although people can

THE 10-STEP BOOK PROCESS

1 - IDEATION
2 - OUTLINE
3 - WRITING
4 - EDITING
5 - COVER DESIGN

6 - INTERIOR LAYOUT
7 - PROOFREADING
8 - BOOK LAUNCH
9 - PRINTING
10 - COMMUNITY

develop unique concepts, those ideas often modify or extend existing ideas. We're not advocating plagiarism; instead, we recognize that the progression of human knowledge depends on building upon the work of others.

It's essential to consider the books and authors that have impacted you. Perhaps you're altering or expanding a concept that's already in circulation. Think about what information or insights you need for the idea to resonate. Chances are, others need that same understanding. Sharing your unique perspective can help those concepts strike home for a new audience.

A common hypothesis in the publishing industry says, "First, write for yourself." Don't chase trends or try to guess what's relevant right now. The writing process is often full of twists and turns, cycles and recursions. If you plan to write your book and pursue traditional publishing, it could be several years before it reaches the world. By that time, current publishing trends may have already faded. So, we recommend writing a book *you* would want to read. Focus on your passion and interests in order to create something that resonates with you.

Finding Your "Somewhere"

Since every book starts with an idea, we can confirm that, despite how many books are in the world, no two books are the same. Each book is written from the author's unique perspective, experience, and expertise.

How do you find your starting point if it could be anywhere on the map? Chances are, you've already seen it. You're likely reading *these* words because there's a book burning inside of you. Stop and think about that for a moment. What is the book about? What do you hear regularly that adds fuel to the fire? Write down some of your thoughts. It doesn't matter if your initial thoughts are disjointed, don't flow, or feel entirely disconnected. Get them out of your head and put them on paper.

If you find this to be an uncomfortable experience, remember that part of the reason those thoughts are still in your head is that they're safe there—and you're protected from what anyone else might say, think, or laugh about if they saw them on a Post-it. We encourage you to be bold and write them down anyway. Once they're on paper, you can strike them, tweak them, or build on them. But you can't do that until you've committed them to paper and created a place to begin.

Perhaps you don't have a specific idea yet, but you have knowledge, expertise, and wisdom to share. Finding a place to start could be as straightforward as reflecting on your interactions with others. What have you said in the past that sparked meaningful conversations or got people thinking? If you have a social media presence, consider starting with a post that made a splash. The same principle applies even if you're not active on social media—think about your professional or personal conversations. What have you shared that captured others' attention and resonated deeply?

Think it through and jot down some ideas. Remember, you don't have to be perfect. Let the sun illuminate your direction, and then commit to getting those ideas on paper!

There are plenty of stages in the writing process that will help you shape these raw thoughts into something publishable and readable. We'll get to those soon. For now, take a breath and congratulate yourself on finding your somewhere.

THE 10-STEP BOOK PROCESS

1 - IDEATION
2 - OUTLINE
3 - WRITING
4 - EDITING
5 - COVER DESIGN
6 - INTERIOR LAYOUT
7 - PROOFREADING
8 - BOOK LAUNCH
9 - PRINTING
10 - COMMUNITY

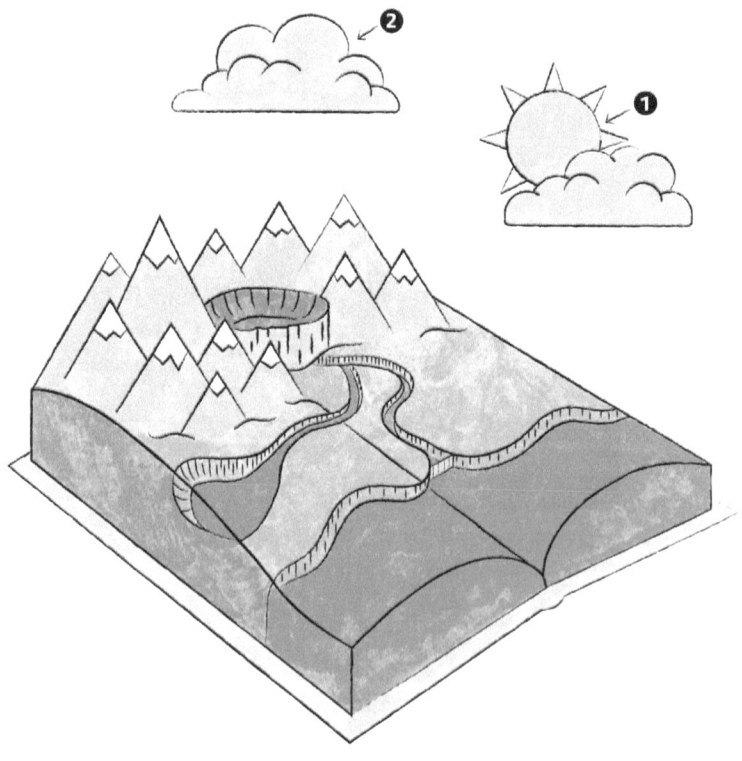

CHAPTER 10

Outline

THE OUTLINE PHASE is represented by clouds that form over the mountain. If you feel like a cloud of your book's thoughts, words, and dreams has formed in your mind, rain is soon to follow. Those drops will form your manuscript when it's all said and done.

First things first: let's talk about the blank page. It's been the terror of so many writers—the scourge of scribes. Vanquishing it is the first step toward taking that dream in your head and making it a reality.

It might not be *easy* to vanquish the blank page, but it is *simple*. You only need to write a few words and then a few more after that. You have a leg up if you've jotted down your ideas. Use those words and phrases to begin writing down your first few lines. The goal for these lines isn't for them to be "good." It's for them to be *there*.

Then, it's time to work on an outline. Before we instruct any of our authors to start writing, we take multiple weeks to focus on creating an outline of the entire book. Yes, we recommend the same step our high school teachers made us take before writing a paper. They emphasized writing an outline for a reason, and so do we. But the fun part is, we're not asking you to write a paper about *Hamlet*. We do not require you to stick with a given format for these many chapters in *that* order. This is your outline for your book. That means you can get creative with it.

There's a fair amount of sifting through the sand to find the gold. Pulling a book out of a big idea isn't easy. That's why we encourage our authors to think through the experiences that have mattered to them *in the context of their ideas*. Which ones do you find yourself repeating? Which ones do you often tell your clients, colleagues, and others in your professional space? Which ones do people seem to respond to the most? If you're writing a memoir, these stories will be your personal experiences that resonate with others. If you're writing non-fiction for a professional space, it might look more like stories demonstrating a thought point. But at their core, they're the same: ideas and experiences to which you keep returning.

Write those down in list form. Don't worry about putting them in a "correct" order at this stage—get them on the page. Now you have a solid starting point for your outline—the clouds are coming together, and rain is on the way!

Your list might need to be longer. Keep thinking and jotting down those experiences and ideas. On the other hand, you might have a list that's three pages long. Congratulations!

You've uncovered the most challenging aspect of writing an outline: choosing what *not* to write about when you want to write about everything.

It's important to recognize that most people have multiple books in them. This is more than just encouragement—it's a helpful way to think about sifting through all the sand of your stories and ideas to find the gold that needs to be in this first book. Once you set aside that gold, you will likely be able to say, "Wow. Not only did I find the gold for this book, but I also found the silver for the next one."

Here's the secret of writing an outline: it's all about figuring out what the book *isn't*. This is where the power of a team comes in—to help you sift through all the sand and recognize the gold (and then help you flesh it out). Once you figure out what this book isn't, you can define what it is. It's like reverse engineering your story to build your book.

It's also much like visiting the optometrist and trying new prescription lenses. You put on that first pair and look at the eye chart. You can make out the colors, but the chart isn't clear. Option two is better. But when you try option three, the whole chart snaps into focus.

Similarly, the first outline you write isn't set in stone. It helps you see some of the elements of your book and indicates what might be missing. With each tweak and "lens change," more and more of your book will come into focus. Getting to the optometrist and trying out that first set of lenses is essential. The outline can be malleable throughout the writing process. It's good to tell yourself that in the beginning so the weight of perfectionism doesn't freeze your effort. Pragmatically speaking, there's a great deal of creativity in writing the outline. Is it an eight-chapter book? A twelve-chapter book? Maybe it's a book with thirty short, explosive chapters. The fun part is it's up to you.

The more time and effort you put into your outline, the more enjoyable the writing process will be. Think of it this way: driving the car somewhere is easier when you know where you're going. You can take in the scenery or change course halfway through if you have a clear roadmap.

Organizing Your Stories

Now that you have a list of your stories and experiences, it's time to think through the best order for each to appear in your book. One common approach is to structure your book linearly, following the order of events. This method works well, especially if you're narrating a sequence of events. However, the challenge with linear organization is that it may require adding extra details or filler content to bridge the gap between each point.

Imagine you've laid out all the components of a formal dinner setting: dishes, silverware, glassware, napkins, and centerpieces. The question becomes: how do you arrange them to create the best dining experience for your guests? Similarly, when structuring your book linearly, consider how each story or experience flows into the next, ensuring readers find a seamless and engaging narrative.

There is an even more effective way to organize your thoughts. Instead of ordering them linearly, consider arranging them around the core of your message. What is the most critical thing your book needs to convey to your readers? Once you identify that, imagine it as the focal point of a ten-week college course or business seminar. What are the key concepts your audience needs to learn each week? Do some of those ideas naturally build upon others?

Imagine the progression from the least complex concepts introduced in week one to the most complex ones explored in week ten. As you arrange your ideas in this manner, step back and observe. Do you sense your book taking shape? This is much like the power of those clouds coming together to perform nature's work: watering the earth.

THE 10-STEP BOOK PROCESS

1 - IDEATION
2 - OUTLINE
3 - WRITING
4 - EDITING
5 - COVER DESIGN

6 - INTERIOR LAYOUT
7 - PROOFREADING
8 - BOOK LAUNCH
9 - PRINTING
10 - COMMUNITY

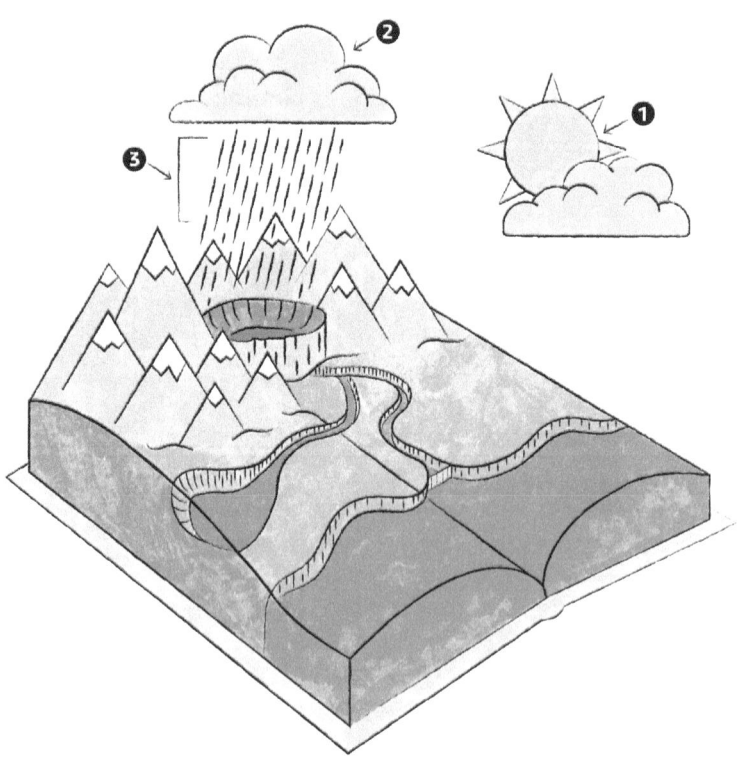

CHAPTER 11

Writing

LET'S ADDRESS ONE of the biggest challenges to the writing process: *time*. In our mountain stream analogy, writing represents the rain. However, a book cannot be written with just a few raindrops—a "drought" is not what we're aiming for. Time is what allows for more rain. If you are short on time, we hope this chapter provides insight into navigating the book-writing process effectively.

How you manage your time in the writing process, the amount of time allocated for writing, and how you structure and safeguard that time will all shape the outcome of your book. The reality for many of our authors who publish with Streamline is that they require more time to dedicate to writing. They are juggling multiple responsibilities, transitioning from a traditional work schedule to dedicating hours to traveling and speaking engagements or reprioritizing to spend more time with their families—all of which are commendable endeavors. However, these commitments often subtract from the available "butt in the seat" writing time.

Writing a book requires sitting down and putting in the work. Rain is what nurtures flowers, fills lakes and rivers, and sustains life on Earth! Does the prospect of sitting down and working on your book sound invigorating or daunting to you? If you lean towards the latter, you're in good company. Many others agree with the axiom 'I hate to write, but I love having written.' Either way, doing the work entails scheduling blocks of time, committing to staying focused for the duration, and making progress step by step.

Writing is the practice of consistency. I must show up in my chair and stay focused on the task at hand. However, there's also room for flexibility in finding a rhythm that works for you. For example, you might thrive with a large block of uninterrupted time to reign in your thoughts and get down to business. On the other hand, you might find that shorter bursts of time suit your style better, allowing you to sprint through a few paragraphs or pages.

If this is your first book, you may not know which option works best for you—and that's okay. Take two weeks and "audition" both options. Neither method is inherently better than the other. The important thing is to find what works best for you and commit to consistently showing up.

Another challenge in the writing process is the presence of too many cooks in the kitchen. While having a team come alongside your book journey is invaluable, striking a balance is essential. Every author benefits from a support system—individuals who can cheer them on, help them try out their ideas, and offer constructive feedback on how they might best tweak their book. But, if this feedback loop becomes too large, it can be a hindrance instead of help.

Getting it Right

Now that you've established your writing schedule and narrowed your feedback circle, it's time to confront the blank page. Are you afraid of making mistakes? The answer is likely yes, as fear of failure is common among writers. Perfectionism is the enemy of excellent writing. Your book does not have to be perfect—it never will be. Embrace imperfection and bring your clay to the table.

You've probably heard of "word vomit," or the process of writing with abandon, without stopping to wonder whether a particular word, phrase, or idea is good enough. Well, that's the clay we're talking about. You cannot create a finished sculpture without first taking a lump of raw clay to the workbench. You cannot create a finished book without first putting raw words on a page.

Bring your clay to the table. It doesn't have to be perfect; in fact, at this point, it shouldn't be. Trust in your ability and in the clay itself. Remember, it's what God gave you to work with in the first place. Once it's there, you can shape, mold, and give it as many turns on the wheel as necessary for it to take form.

Getting in Flow

Entering a flow state means your attention is absorbed in the task. It's a place of deep focus, where the rest of the world disappears, and you effortlessly generate ideas. Being in flow is enjoyable and often energizing. Tasks don't feel like chores; they become immersive experiences. Ideally, you would enter a flow state every time you write, but that is not always possible. However, you increase the chance of entering this highly productive state by approaching it with intention.

Plan Your Flow

Schedule time on your calendar for deep work and entering the flow state. Block out these periods as distraction-free hours. In a world of emails, texts, and app notifications, getting caught up in important but non-urgent tasks takes a lot of work, preventing us from fully immersing ourselves in the flow. Train yourself to view these hours as necessary, urgent times—and protect them accordingly.

Get Your Mind Right

Successful athletes excel at listening to positive talks, messages, and music to get hyped for practice or a game. Similarly, find what boosts your mood and engages your brain. Settle down in a neatly arranged physical space, listen to a playlist, or even have a favorite beverage beside you—each can signal to your brain that it's game time.

Be Consistent

Consistency is key when staying in the manuscript for a set amount each day. While it might seem appealing to dedicate an entire day to writing, it's often more practical to spread your writing sessions over shorter, regular intervals. If an all-day writing session works for you, then go for it. Strive to find what works best and stick with it.

Just as rain nourishes the earth and brings life to the land, your words have the power to inspire, inform, and uplift others. Every drop of your story contributes to the greater flow of human knowledge and understanding. So, let your words pour forth like rain, filling streams of thought and imagination and enriching the world with your unique perspective. Even if your impact seems small at first, remember that every drop counts, and together, they can create a mighty river of inspiration.

THE 10-STEP BOOK PROCESS

1 - IDEATION
2 - OUTLINE
3 - WRITING
4 - EDITING
5 - COVER DESIGN
6 - INTERIOR LAYOUT
7 - PROOFREADING
8 - BOOK LAUNCH
9 - PRINTING
10 - COMMUNITY

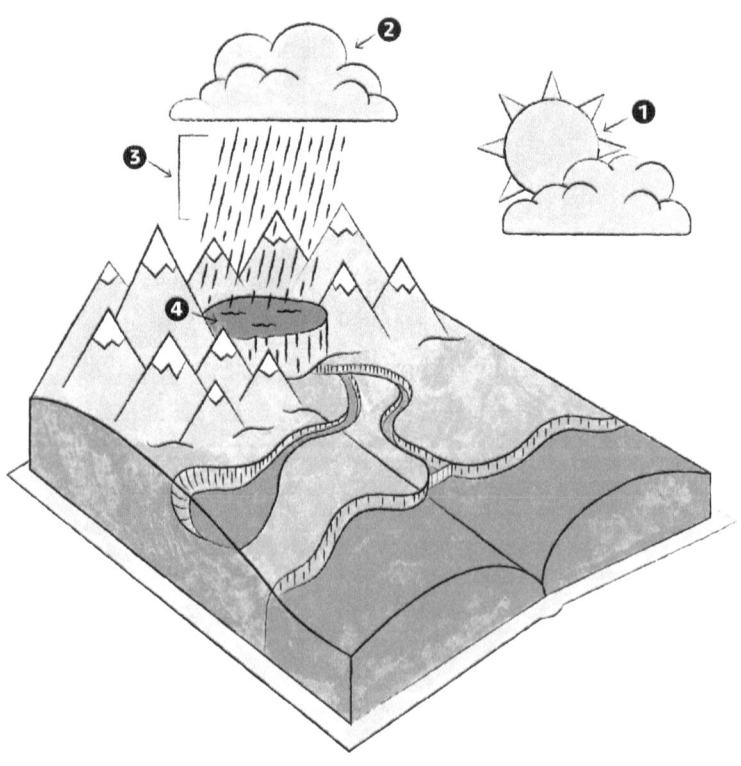

CHAPTER 12

Don't Seek to Get Published; Seek to Get Edited

ONCE THE RAIN hits the earth's foundation, surface runoff takes place. Surface runoff in the editing process separates the words that will be included in your final manuscript and those to be left behind. In other words, not all rain gets to flow into the river and ocean.

Author James K. Smith once said, "You want to be a writer? In our day and age, it's easy to 'get published.' Set higher goals: hope to be edited."

If there's one thing that dovetails with our message in this book, it's precisely that. To unpack what he means, let's return to our clay-to-the-table analogy.

Can the lump of clay be brought to the table, moved to a pedestal as-is, and called finished? History will tell you it can.

DON'T SEEK TO GET *published,* SEEK TO GET *edited*

A quick Google search will yield photos of Marcel Duchamp's readymade sculpture, *Fountain*, which is nothing more than a urinal (yes, you read that right) that the artist displayed after inscribing it with a signature and year. Duchamp's sculpture initiated an entirely new artistic movement known as *avant-garde*. He landed himself on the art world's equivalent of a bestseller list.

But what if your goal isn't to disrupt the art world but to create a beautiful thrown-pottery vase or bowl instead? That requires a different set of tools and skills. You'll need your clay, but you'll also need a pottery wheel and an instructor. Otherwise, the most likely outcome is that you will set your clay spinning, and the entire lump will splatter on a nearby wall.

When someone who already has the skills to work the wheel and mold the clay comes alongside you, suddenly, you have the means to craft something beautiful, functional, and meaningful for the people who need it. Remember, some people need to hear your story and *expertise. The world needs your book.*

What the world needs less is more *content*. Content creation has its advantages. It's quick, of the moment, and often can be done with little to no financial investment. Creating art, on the other hand, is very different. It might not seem like it took much time or effort for our friend Marcel Duchamp to "create" his sculpture, but remember, he spent over a decade honing his artistic voice and style before *Fountain* ever existed. Then, when he had something important to share with the world, he poured all that learned experience and expertise into his art.

What happened next? Duchamp connected with his world. He reached the people who needed to hear what he had to say. Over a hundred years later, his work continues to connect.

Will we still discuss some memes and social media videos in a hundred years? Sure. Will some of them be considered art? Perhaps. But most online content won't find the kind of lasting audience or impact that a book can. Writing a book is about creating something enduring, something that resonates and connects with people across time.

So, bring your clay, your story, and your expertise. Let's craft something beautiful together. Your book has the potential to leave a legacy, to be the piece of art that people turn to for inspiration, knowledge, and connection long after the latest online trends have faded away.

Then why should you seek to get edited? Because refining and crafting your message is essential. It is the difference between creating content and crafting a piece of art. If you want to connect with the past, present, and future, you owe it to the people who need to hear what you have to say to present your message thoughtfully and thoroughly. You owe it to them to make it the best it can be.

You owe it to yourself, too. You're stepping out in courage, bringing your clay to the table, and vouching for its value. Follow up on that boldness with careful craftsmanship and bring someone alongside you who can help you scrape away the excess and reveal the message only your story can convey. An editor can be that skilled partner, helping you turn a rough draft into a polished masterpiece, ensuring your unique voice and vision shine through.

Here's another reason to get your work edited. You might aspire to see your writing in a magazine, a newspaper published online, or in print, but none of that matters if your content is sub-par. No one wants a soup bowl full of holes. Sometimes, you can be so close to your project that you fail to see its flaws. You might even overlook the holes themselves.

Like a pottery instructor, an editor provides a fresh perspective, helping you identify and fix issues you might have missed. They ensure your message is clear, your arguments are solid, and your prose is polished. In short, they help you present your best work to the world.

An editor can spot problems quickly and reliably. Trust us when we say you always need a second pair of eyes on your writing. We have professional editors to review our work for each book we publish—our own and those of our Streamline authors. We believe in our system and the power of a team coming together so strongly that we used the exact "Turnkey Publishing Process" to create the book you're reading. We can say with the utmost confidence that we don't just *think* our process works—we *know* it does. We've seen it succeed for our authors and ourselves so often that we wouldn't consider creating a book any other way.

As you continue writing, you may need to tweak your outline as the book evolves. That's okay! Much of the writing process is about discovery. However, it's essential not to let that evolution take you too far off course. Did you uncover a brilliant new facet of your message while writing? Amazing!

Give it a moment to breathe, then return to your original outline. Ask yourself: Where does it fit? Is it a natural extension of your main idea? Is it necessary for your readers to fully understand or absorb the concept? Or are you trying to shoehorn it in somewhere?

If it fits naturally, tweak your outline and integrate it into your book. If it doesn't quite fit or would require significant effort to incorporate, consider saving it for your next project. If you're uncertain about whether it belongs, consult your team. Like a seasoned pottery instructor, they'll likely have great instincts about whether and where to include it.

Types of Editing

Editing falls into two main types: developmental and grammatical editing. They are very different, and each serves an essential purpose in the evolution of your book.

> **DEVELOPMENTAL EDITING** is high-level editing after you've drafted an outline and written significant portions or complete drafts of your book. The focus isn't on commas, typos, or run-on sentences at this stage. Instead, your editor will concentrate on whether your ideas are fully developed, coherent within the context of your message, and supported by sufficient evidence. They will also assess whether your stories and examples are structured to build momentum, engage readers, and ultimately form a cohesive and compelling narrative.

In many ways, developmental editing is the "heavy lifting" stage of editing. It is often challenging for a writer to handle their own developmental edit. Because they already have all the information about their topic in mind, it can be difficult to spot gaps that might confuse their readers. Bringing in a fresh set of eyes is invaluable.

A good developmental edit will resolve any big issues in your book that could cause readers to put it down. A great developmental edit will keep them hungry for more.

GRAMMATICAL EDITING, on the other hand, is ground-level editing. It happens after you and your developmental editor are confident that your content is fully realized and well-organized. At this stage of editing, often called a line or copy edit, the focus shifts to those commas, typos, and run-on sentences. An editor will meticulously comb through the manuscript, line by line, correcting grammar and punctuation. They will also suggest changes to improve the book's readability, ensuring it flows smoothly. Professional editors adhere to established standards like the Chicago Manual of Style or APA.

Whether grammatical editing feels like "heavy lifting" or not depends on the individual writer. Simply put, we don't know what we don't know. That's why it's wise to bring in someone else for this detailed editing work once you've taken the manuscript as far as it can go on your own.

A good grammatical edit will resolve any errors that, when spotted by a reader, can undermine the book's credibility. A great grammatical edit will enhance readability, highlighting your story and ideas.

These rounds of editing are crucial to ensure the best content flows seamlessly into the final manuscript. Streamline developmental editors and ghostwriters will evaluate and adjust your book's structure, coherence, and momentum. Then, a grammatical editor meticulously follows up to polish the text. While no book is perfect, having two sets of professional eyes, in addition to your own, significantly increases the likelihood of catching errors and enhancing quality.

It's essential to involve only a few people in the editing process. Having too many cooks in the kitchen can complicate and dilute your vision. Editing by family members, while well-intentioned, can be risky for various reasons. Instead, find someone skilled and honest who will provide the constructive feedback necessary to make your book the best it can be.

CHAPTER 13

Cover Design

IMAGINE THE MOST beautiful waterfall you have ever seen—not just a picture-perfect scene from a Google image. Hopefully, you've had the privilege of standing before a natural waterfall and experiencing its awe-inspiring majesty firsthand. Whether it's the grandeur of Niagara Falls or the tranquility of a secluded cascade along a wooded trail, witnessing a waterfall in person is a captivating experience.

From a visual standpoint, we aim for your book cover to evoke the same sense of wonder and fascination. We've all heard the saying, "You can't judge a book by its cover," and it's wise advice when applied to individuals. As we move through this life, it's crucial to remember that what's inside a person counts. So, in that respect, the saying is true.

When it comes to *actual* books, the cover plays a crucial role. At first glance, a book's cover is all we have to go on. We're far more likely to reach for a book with a cover that

THE 10-STEP BOOK PROCESS

1 - IDEATION
2 - OUTLINE
3 - WRITING
4 - EDITING
5 - COVER DESIGN
6 - INTERIOR LAYOUT
7 - PROOFREADING
8 - BOOK LAUNCH
9 - PRINTING
10 - COMMUNITY

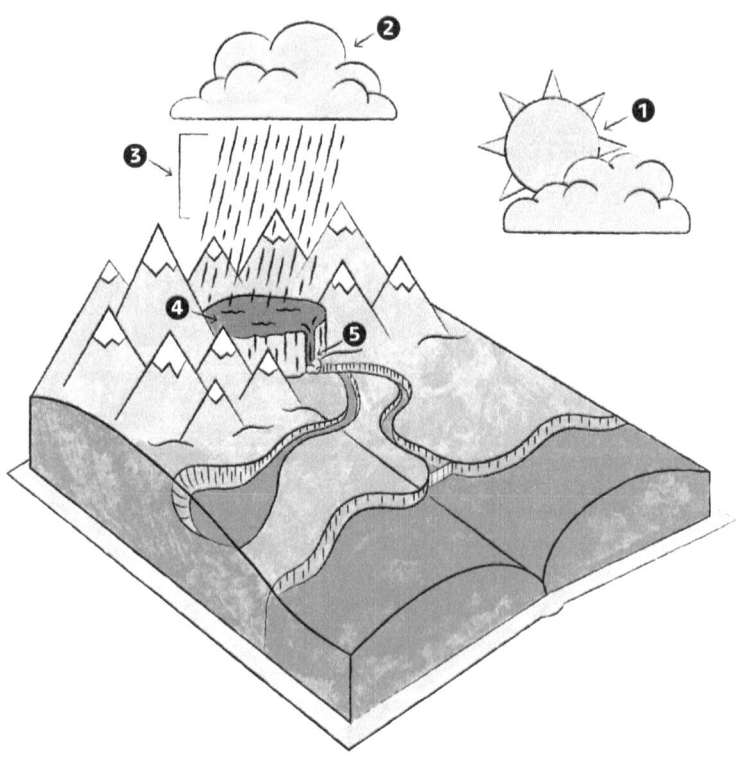

speaks to us in some way and just as likely to pass over one that gives the wrong impression.

What cover are you most likely to reach for? Chances are, it'll be eye-catching and striking. The imagery, font, and colors impart a specific feeling or tone that captures your attention. So, while they say you can't judge a book by its cover, the reality is that we often do.

In other words, good design matters. The cover design communicates your book to a potential reader. After all the time and effort spent writing, editing, and everything else that goes into publication, make sure the cover conveys the right message. Great design will help ensure your book's cover enhances, rather than hinders, your book sales.

Be Bold

When it comes to cover design, do yourself a favor by adding an element that feels fresh and bold. That's not to say you should go so far out on a design limb that it breaks off the tree, but the strongest covers incorporate boldness in some way. Boldness comes through the risk-taking that sets you apart from the other books in your space.

Here's the good news: whether you realize it or not, you already practice that kind of boldness. Here's what we mean. You're writing a book because you're bold enough to say something that hasn't already been said before and tell a story that's uniquely yours. All you need to do now is translate that boldness into your cover design.

So, think about the audience. What do they need to see on the cover to know the book is for them? Design with your audience in mind by letting those elements directly translate to the cover.

Your design should communicate your book's branding, ideas, and tone. The visual cues—colors, fonts, images, and graphics—should look and feel like they come from the same place as the book. If you have personal or business branding, you'll want to incorporate elements in your cover design to create a cohesive look that ties everything together.

Just like your outline, it's more likely your cover design will require multiple iterations. While a basic design may suffice initially, exploring versions two and three is always a good idea. Trying out different tweaks in those versions allows you to take risks and assess their impact. Which version exudes boldness? Which version snaps your book into focus? Which one communicates your book's message best?

Consider what else you've seen or appreciated. We often advise authors that while there may be nothing entirely new under the sun, there's always room for innovation, especially in your book and its cover design. No one else will write your manuscript word for word, nor will they craft the same cover with identical fonts, colors, and image arrangements.

This realization can alleviate some of the pressure. With countless books and covers already in existence, which elements do you like? Which ones capture your attention? Take a mental inventory and play around with those elements. Perhaps it's a font from one book, a color scheme from another, and graphics from a third. What emerges when combined with your story and ideas? Often, this blending leads to the creation of an initial cover design. In essence, the contributions you bring to the table directly shape the gorgeous waterfall that follows.

No two waterfalls are alike–each possesses unique beauty and character. Similarly, like a waterfall, your book is a distinctive creation, yours to unveil to the world. Whether it becomes a towering cascade or a gentle stream, its beauty will captivate those who behold it.

THE 10-STEP BOOK PROCESS

1 - IDEATION
2 - OUTLINE
3 - WRITING
4 - EDITING
5 - COVER DESIGN

6 - INTERIOR LAYOUT
7 - PROOFREADING
8 - BOOK LAUNCH
9 - PRINTING
10 - COMMUNITY

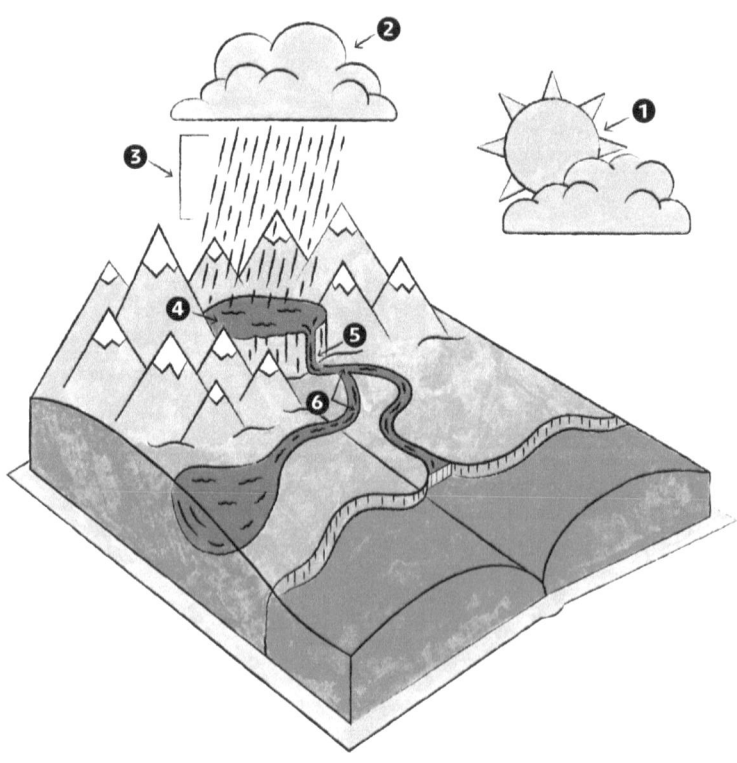

CHAPTER 14

Interior Layout/Design

INTERIOR AND LAYOUT design—including typesetting—is its own kind of art. Just as a waterfall offers an ethereal experience, rivers and lakes are equally beautiful. In the same way, a book's interior design can be as captivating as its cover, enhancing the reader's overall experience.

Like grammar, mechanics, and style conventions, professional interior and layout design follows specific rules, like APA or Chicago style, governing its deployment in any given book. People can sometimes follow those rules to create their interior layout, but they must first know them.

Let's take a step back. What is interior layout design and typesetting?

> **INTERIOR LAYOUT DESIGN** refers to organizing the visual and typographic elements within a book's pages. This includes decisions about margins, font styles and sizes,

typesetting, headers, call-out boxes, and line spacing. The goal is to create a visually appealing and readable book that enhances the reader's experience.

TYPESETTING is a subset of interior design focused on text arrangement on the page. It involves font, typeface, spacing between the words and letters, symbols, and glyphs. Typesetting helps to optimize the reading experience further, ensuring the text flows smoothly from page to page.

Both interior layout design and typesetting are essential components of book production. When done well, they can elevate a book's quality and professionalism.

In book design, the interior layout is organized into three main categories: front matter, manuscript, and back matter. Each section plays a crucial role in the overall structure and presentation of the book.

A book's **FRONT MATTER** consists of everything before the manuscript begins, including the title page, copyright page, dedication, forward, preface, acknowledgments, table of contents, and introduction.

The **MANUSCRIPT** is the book's main body, beginning with Chapter One and continuing to the final chapter. This is the core content of your book, where your main message, story, or information is presented. Each chapter should be well-organized and formatted consistently to ensure a smooth reading experience.

The **BACK MATTER** includes everything that appears after the manuscript ends. This section often includes an afterword, acknowledgments, appendices, glossary, references, and index.

Once the content of those elements is ready to go, it's time to begin your design.

Why are Interior Layout Design and Typesetting Important?

When done well, interior layout designs and typesetting enhance the reader's experience with a book—similar to how a beautifully arranged plate makes food taste better. Conversely, when done haphazardly, they compromise a reader's experience with the book, much like food slopped onto a plate can make you second-guess whether it's worth eating. Because these elements influence the reader's experience, they can also affect your book's sales.

In some ways, typesetting could be defined as "how not to lose your reader" or "how to make sure your reader comprehends your ideas." Typesetting involves removing anything from the page that will distract your reader, cause them to pause, interfere with their reading comprehension, or give them a reason to stop reading your book. After working so hard to get your book into the reader's hands, you don't want them to put it down because of the words' *appearance* on the page.

Think of it this way: No news is good news about interior design layout and typesetting. Readers shouldn't have questions about the book's interior design and typesetting because it should be seamless and seem effortless—invisible. That's when you know your interior layout design is a knockout.

Certain typesetting elements, such as block quotes and ornamental breaks like a star or flower separating a chapter or section, can stick out. These visual cues can also designate specific things or help paint an overall picture of the experience you want a reader to have with your book. Ideally, your *words* paint ninety-nine percent of the picture. Any visual cues only enhance those words.

Returning to our food metaphor: When did you last sit down to a three- or four-course meal and walk away talking about the spices instead of the food? Sometimes, you may comment on a type or combination of spices you haven't tasted before. But if the meal succeeds, you'll say, "That was the best steak I ever had. Can you believe the strawberry cheesecake? Wow."

That's the kind of reaction you want for your book. Rather than having readers focus on section breaks or font size, you want them to view the book as a cohesive and impactful work. Aim for feedback like: "That was one of the best books I've ever read, and now I see X, Y, and Z in an entirely new way." The goal is to create an experience so smooth and engaging that the design elements fade into the background, immersing your readers in your story or message.

Team Typesetting

Historically, interior design layouts and typesetting have been tied up with printing presses. These presses used individual blocks with raised letters and symbols set tightly into frames.

A page was born once the surface of the blocks was inked and paper pressed between them.

These days, typesetting is more digital than physical. Instead of using a set of blocks, a frame to hold the type together, bottles of ink, and pressure to transfer inked impressions to paper, you only need a computer and a typesetting program. One person can manage the entire process. However, we encourage you to bring a small group of trusted individuals to help. The team members must know the typesetting rules to help you create an excellent "meal" of your book that will enrich readers through your words and content—not its ancillary components.

Working with a team brings valuable perspectives and ensures your book's interior design is polished and professional. Team members knowledgeable in typesetting can help you navigate the complexities of font choices, spacing, margins, and other layout elements. Their input can make the difference between a good book and a great one, where the design enhances the reader's experience without distracting from the content.

Ultimately, just as the world's water systems are interconnected and flow together harmoniously, the interior of your book should feel cohesive. Nothing about the look and feel of your book should feel disjointed. Instead, every element should support your core message and the story you want to share with the world.

THE 10-STEP BOOK PROCESS

1 - IDEATION
2 - OUTLINE
3 - WRITING
4 - EDITING
5 - COVER DESIGN
6 - INTERIOR LAYOUT
7 - PROOFREADING
8 - BOOK LAUNCH
9 - PRINTING
10 - COMMUNITY

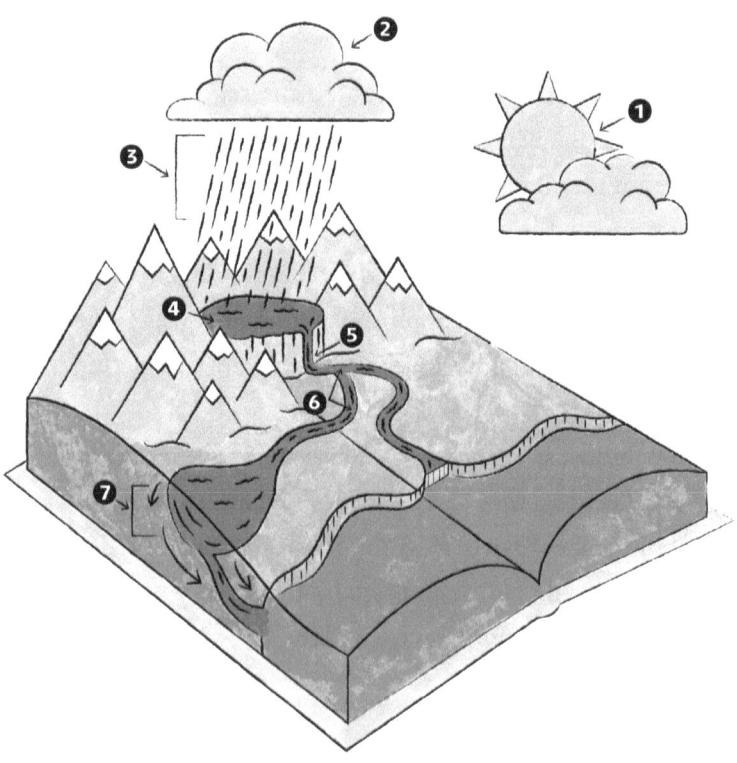

CHAPTER 15

Proofreading

BY NOW, YOU know we are big advocates for getting multiple sets of eyes on a manuscript before publication. However, we also acknowledge that doing so can challenge some authors. This is why we view proofreading as groundwater flow. Just as groundwater flows through soil and earth, proofreading circulates through your manuscript, refining it like water nourishing the land. Just as all water that falls to the earth eventually joins rivers, streams, lakes, and waterfalls; similarly, all editing input shapes your final draft.

Imposter syndrome and the fear of vulnerability often keep authors from seeking outside feedback. It takes courage to accept the advice of others. Even when surrounded by knowledgeable, supportive writing and editing professionals, sharing your work can be daunting. However, getting their advice is invaluable in shaping your manuscript into its best form.

Let's dive into that necessity. As an author, you carefully, exhilaratingly, and painstakingly work to craft your book for readers. All the planning and effort—from exploring your first idea to strategizing your launch and book sale efforts—aims to give your reader a seamless reading experience. However, spelling errors, grammatical mistakes, and typos can disrupt this flow and detract from your message. If left unaddressed, these errors risk undermining your authority on the subject and tarnishing the reader's perception of your work.

Another way to put it is to emphasize the importance of completing the proofreading step. Whether you're embarking on the book journey independently or with the support of a service like Streamline, we encourage you to dedicate adequate time and resources to proofreading.

As You Proofread

Proofreading is the final editing step before publication. At this point, your content and style have undergone thorough editing. You should be confident that you've effectively conveyed your message, organized your ideas logically, and used appropriate language. Completing the writing step beforehand will save you time because it prevents you from proofreading multiple times.

Running your document through spell check, AI, and online proofreading services is a great starting point. These programs can catch obvious spelling errors and typos but aren't foolproof. It's common to see a manuscript deemed "clean" by one of these programs still needing extensive work—sometimes costing thousands of dollars in corrections. Carefully read your book from cover to cover to ensure all the errors are caught and corrected.

As mentioned earlier, we don't know what we don't know. Similarly, you can't catch an error you don't recognize if you're not entirely confident in grammar, spelling, punctuation, and other proofreading nuances. It's crucial to take the time to refresh your knowledge. This could involve revisiting grammar guides, style manuals, or online resources to ensure you're well-equipped to catch and correct any errors in your writing.

If you hire a professional proofreader, familiarize yourself with their credentials, turnaround time, and fees. Ask for a quote before you engage their services, keeping in mind that the complexity and needs of your manuscript will affect the overall cost and timeline.

Finding the right person to bring to your writing project is often difficult. When rain falls to the ground, groundwater flow takes over, a natural process ensuring the water's journey continues smoothly. Similarly, having a team in your corner to guide you through the editing process from start to finish can make the entire journey feel just as natural and seamless.

THE 10-STEP BOOK PROCESS

1 - IDEATION
2 - OUTLINE
3 - WRITING
4 - EDITING
5 - COVER DESIGN
6 - INTERIOR LAYOUT
7 - PROOFREADING
8 - BOOK LAUNCH
9 - PRINTING
10 - COMMUNITY

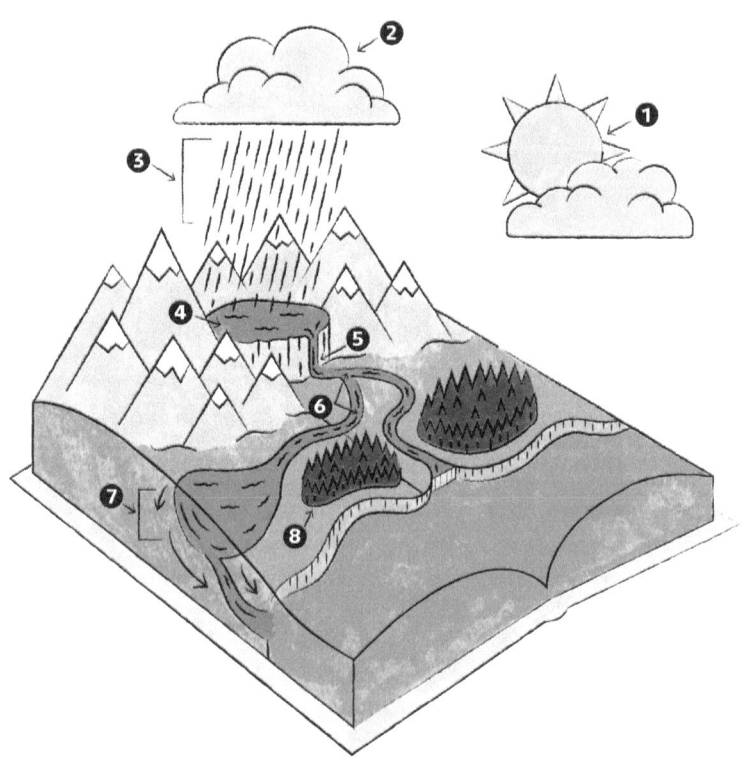

CHAPTER 16

Book Launch

WHEN YOU SEE green grass, it symbolizes life and thriving nature. Similarly, embarking on your book launch after publishing signifies the culmination of all the effort and groundwork you've put in—the rain of ideas, the flow of writing, and now the growth of your book. Just like the green grass indicates the success of the preceding natural processes, your book launch is a testament to the culmination of your hard work, marking the beginning of a new chapter where your message can flourish and reach its intended audience.

We understand that many details must be addressed when publishing and selling a book. It's never been easier to publish a book but never harder to sell one. That's why we focus on facing the challenge head-on.

Selling books is hard work, so solid writing, editing, proofreading, and design are critical. Streamline exists to bring an incredible team around your dream—helping you achieve the professional results needed to bring your book to life. We also have excellent partners ready to support you. But after those stages are complete, many of our authors want to know how we can help with the aftermath of their book entering the market. This is where our growing author community comes into play.

Gasoline vs. Kindling

There's so much emphasis in the publishing industry on a book's launch. Traditional and professional publishers alike put together book launch kits. Don't get us wrong. We love a great launch. Bringing a book into the world should be a fun, celebratory moment, and we encourage you to do just that! But let's be honest: those brief moments of excitement often translate into the expectation of runaway book sales.

What happens when gasoline is thrown on a fire? After the initial flare of huge flames and intense heat, you're left with a fire that quickly burns out. That's why we are less interested in gasoline and far more passionate to help authors form kindling and craft the base for a longer-lasting fire. That's the inverse of gasoline. That's saying, "Yes, we might need to invest time gathering sticks for a while, but that's okay. We're going to be here longer. We're building a fire that will last longer and provide warmth for future generations."

Our goal is to provide authors with post-launch resources to set them up for long-term success that builds steadily and consistently over time. You'll find many of these resources within our growing community! You could think of each resource as a stick to gather and build your fire—writing an email newsletter, creating posts on social media, or starting a podcast to share your material. You'll find an entire checklist at the end of this chapter. It's our fire starter kit—one we believe is much more than a can of gasoline. We hope it will spark new ideas for your post-launch path forward.

While we're on the subject, there's one more myth we want to dismantle: overnight success is not usually accomplished *overnight*. It may look like someone's book, album, or promotion came out of nowhere, but ask any of those individuals, and they'll tell you about all the months, years, or even decades of consistent, invisible work that led them to their "moment." As Will's mentor says, "You don't have to boil the ocean tomorrow." Nowhere is that more true than authoring, publishing, and shepherding your book post-launch. A book journey is a marathon, not a sprint. Cliché or not, that's just *true*.

The effort you put into the journey is what you will get out of it. If you put twenty percent effort into moving copies of your book, speaking, and growing your business, you will generally see twenty percent growth in return. For many of our authors, that works. They come to the process knowing they don't need to sell hundreds or thousands of copies. Other authors are genuinely motivated to sell as many books as possible. That's equally great. They put seventy or eighty percent into selling books and often see that kind of return.

Still, we encourage our authors to be realistic about their book sales. Reframing expectations about writing a bestseller means accepting that, once your book is on the internet, it's one among millions. Unless you are part of the 0.0001 percent who have already built massive platforms and have a devoted fan base, publishing your book will not make you an overnight celebrity. Unless you are a high-profile celebrity, selling thousands of copies monthly is not the norm. That's okay because you get to do something even more meaningful: write the book you were born to write and share your message with the people who need to hear it.

Bear the Torch, Scatter the Seeds

When it comes to the launch, understanding the various avenues you can use to get your book into the hands of readers is crucial. Email, newsletters, websites, blogs, social media posts, and in-person events are all pathways to connect with those who need your book. Equally important is defining what success means to you and taking responsibility for making it happen. This means believing in your message and recognizing that you must be the torch bearer. Accept the effort to reach the people who need it and do everything you can to share it.

That doesn't mean you should try to do everything, everywhere, all at once. A book about underwater basket weaving isn't likely to find its primary audience in leadership training. Instead, be strategic about where you feel called to make an impact and focus your efforts in those areas with those individuals. Position yourself in environments where your message will resonate with the people who will most benefit from it.

Being strategic includes more than just choosing the right places to be—it's also about deciding what actions to take. This applies explicitly to speaking at free events and giving away copies of your book. People are often afraid to give their books away, but we do it all the time. Part of our commitment is to add value for others. We don't expect anything in return—we hand someone a book and hope they'll benefit from it.

Simply put, it's our job to scatter the seeds. It's the only way that green grass will grow, and only God knows what will come of it. Who might benefit from a free copy of your book? How could an unpaid speaking engagement encourage someone else? When you are willing to make small sacrifices and make yourself available, you'll likely be blown away by the results.

Keep Traveling

Remember, publishing a book is not the "arrival." Instead, it marks the beginning of your authorship journey. So, keep traveling beyond the launch. Bring the same intentionality and endurance to this stage as you did to the writing, editing, design, and publishing process. Doing so will unlock incredible doors and realize your book's full potential.

In your authorship journey, here is kindling to light your fire:

WRITE YOUR BOOK. This is the hardest part, and you did it! We're proud of your accomplishment and cannot wait to hear testimonials about how others benefit from your excellent work.

SET A LAUNCH DATE. The most vulnerable thing you can do is push through Resistance to release your message into the world. Persevere, and you will be amazed by the impact of your courage.

ORDER AUTHOR COPIES. We will provide step-by-step instructions on ordering author copies to sell and sign for others. Make sure others pay you for your work.

TELL FRIENDS AND FAMILY. Your friends and family might be your biggest cheerleaders throughout your book launch process. Show them how to buy, review, and share your book.

CREATE AN ENGAGING UNBOXING VIDEO. Unboxing videos receive great feedback and engagement. Show the world a video of opening your box of books for the first time, and share the message of why you wrote it.

USE SOCIAL MEDIA. Create a social media content schedule to promote your book and send messages consistently on these platforms.

SEND AN EMAIL BLAST. An email subscriber list is just as, if not more, important than a social media presence. Start by creating your email list and use it to promote your new book.

ASK FOR TESTIMONIALS. Ask friends and family for testimonials about your book. These endorsements will be crucial as others engage with your content and message, boosting overall engagement.

PROVIDE FREE SPEAKING EVENTS. Many authors opt for free speaking engagements to promote their books. This marketing strategy not only helps you distribute books on a larger scale but also has the potential to transition into paid opportunities over time.

SECURE LOCAL TV AND RADIO SPOTS. Email local producers with a link to your new book and let them know you'd love to come on their show. Offer free copies of your book in exchange for an interview opportunity.

SEND HANDWRITTEN NOTES. Write a list of fifty leaders you know and send them a free copy of your book with a handwritten note stating how much you would love to share your message with their team.

SEND DIRECT MESSAGES. Successful authors regularly send out direct messages to prospects about their books. Aim to send ten direct messages per business day—and ensure you consistently follow through.

WRITE A REGULAR NEWSLETTER. Create a newsletter that updates your subscribers about your book and launch. Grow your subscriber base and set yourself up well for future book launches!

CREATE A WEBSITE. As an author and speaker, it is essential to have a professional-looking website that people see when they search for you online. Invest in a quality site.

PURSUE PODCASTS. Establish the habit of contacting podcasters to share your message. Utilize cold emails and direct messages to reach out to podcast hosts. Additionally, think about launching your own podcast to expand your reach and share your message with a broader audience.

GIVE AWAYS BOOKS. Sharing your book with someone you've just met can be incredibly fulfilling and is a tangible way to provide value to others. Additionally, consider hosting book giveaways on social media platforms to generate excitement and interest in your book.

TAKE SPEAKING PHOTOS AND VIDEOS. Capture photos and videos of yourself delivering speeches about your book and recording the content of your presentations. These visuals are great for your website and social media channels, offering a glimpse of you in action.

SET MONTHLY GOALS. Establish monthly goals to drive your book promotion efforts. Consider objectives such as the number of speaking engagements you aim to secure or the number of podcasts you target for guest appearances. Setting these goals will help drive momentum and ultimately contribute to increased book sales.

IMPACT "ONE" PERSON. This is the "hidden impact" you can experience. Touching just one person's life can have a profound ripple effect, and this impact often goes unnoticed. Your book and message could potentially transform each individual you reach. Your responsibility is to consistently show up and strive to make a positive difference, trusting that even impacting one person can create a significant change in the world.

STAY ENCOURAGED. Maintain your motivation and enthusiasm. It's worth celebrating your achievement in publishing and launching your book, considering that most people aspire to write a book, but only a fraction ever accomplish it. You have achieved a fantastic feat by publishing and launching your book into the world! Your dedication and perseverance have led you to this significant milestone.

PROMOTE OTHERS. Promoting a book is fun but hard work. One of the best ways to find success is by encouraging others. Connect with like-minded authors and support one another regularly.

KNOW YOUR MATERIAL. Read your book repeatedly so you are familiar with the content. People will ask about specific parts or reference details they liked. Always have an answer prepared.

REPURPOSE CONTENT. Utilize your book's content creatively by repurposing it across various platforms and formats. Extract critical principles and insights from your book to develop action plans, group studies, or other resources that resonate with your audience. By repurposing your content, you can extend its reach and impact, engaging your audience in diverse and meaningful ways.

WRITE BOOK TWO! We can't wait to help write your next book and the one after that!

THE 10-STEP BOOK PROCESS

1 - IDEATION
2 - OUTLINE
3 - WRITING
4 - EDITING
5 - COVER DESIGN
6 - INTERIOR LAYOUT
7 - PROOFREADING
8 - BOOK LAUNCH
9 - PRINTING
10 - COMMUNITY

CHAPTER 17

Printing

IN OUR MOUNTAIN stream graphic, the ocean represents something vast and never-ending. Your ideas, thoughts, and words have journeyed through an incredible life cycle—now, they are ready to transition from a flowing stream into the boundless world ahead. The ocean awaits, and while it can be daunting, with the right guide, it becomes a fascinating adventure.

Publishing your book is just one part of the process. While publishing is the short-term solution to bringing your book to life, high-quality printing is the long-term answer to ensure your book reaches its audience.

A Word on Publishing

Before we delve into the crucial topic of printing, we want to guide you through the various facets of publishing. Over the years, we've had the incredible opportunity to speak with and learn from our authors. Many aspects of what we do at Streamline have grown from those invaluable conversations. This is especially true when understanding the challenges authors face when writing a book on their own.

In these conversations, coordinating and completing all the steps to bring a book to life while maintaining creativity and focus invariably comes up. Authors often face the dilemma of deciding which tasks to outsource and finding trustworthy, skilled professionals to handle those tasks when the process feels overwhelming.

If that sounds like a lot, it's because it is, especially the last step. Without a solid level of familiarity with the publishing world, and sometimes even with it, outsourcing can feel like hiring someone you don't know or trust. You hope the person you hire will get the job done and their skills match their resume.

That's why we're so proud of our Turnkey Publishing solution. We've worked hard to solve those pain points for our authors and create a trustworthy, seamless process from beginning to end. Let's dive into what an author can reasonably expect to encounter as they navigate the publishing landscape.

Choosing a Publisher (and Avoiding Publishing Scams in the Process)

Knowledge is power. In the publishing world, a little clarity can go a long way in helping authors choose the path to publication that best suits their goals and helps them avoid falling victim to a scam. Unfortunately, our industry also has its share of people and "companies" that follow unethical or even blatantly fraudulent practices. Consider this section a toolkit for making great choices while avoiding bad situations.

First up: some quick definitions.

> **TRADITIONAL PUBLISHER.** Traditional publishing involves established publishing "houses" that handle all aspects of bringing a book to the marketplace. In-house teams of professionals manage the creative, marketing, and distribution work, leveraging their vast network of connections to get your book into stores nationwide. These publishers purchase the rights to exclusively publish, market, and sell an author's work (think terms like "book deal" and "advances"). They don't accept unsolicited manuscripts, so authors who attempt traditional publishing need an agent. Only a fraction of the books submitted are accepted, and the process from agent to publishing contract to final editing to distribution can take years.
>
> On the bright side, traditional publishers shoulder all the financial risks of bringing a book into the world,

including creative, printing, and distribution costs. In exchange, authors keep a much smaller percentage of their book's profits. Traditional publishers focus on making a book marketable and aim to generate significant returns through bestseller status. Consequently, authors lose much creative control over their books, from cover to content.

SELF-PUBLISHING SERVICE. A "self-publishing service" is an umbrella term for publishers who provide a range of professional editorial, design, and marketing services to authors willing to pay upfront for those services. Authors who choose a self-publishing service retain much more creative control and almost all the profits from their book. At Streamline, our turnkey publishing process is a hybrid solution between traditional and self-publishing. We believe it offers the best of both worlds: while we provide marketing services to help authors elevate their message and create a professional product, we take pride in not taking any author royalties, unlike many other book publishing companies.

Self-publishing services offer a wide variety of services from one to the next. Some focus more on creative processes and less on marketing, while others focus on marketing, outreach, and distribution services. There is also a sizable range of professionalism and skill across this arm of the publishing industry. Self-publishing is sometimes called independent publishing, author-assisted publishing, or entrepreneurial publishing.

VANITY PUBLISHING has earned itself a bad rap. Like self-publishing services, vanity publishers charge a fee to produce a book, but these fees are often exorbitant and aimed at making a profit for the vanity press. In their efforts to profit from authors rather than the books, vanity publishers also secure exclusive publishing rights from the author. Although there are exceptions, most vanity publishers are more concerned with making a profit than delivering a quality book to the world.

Many vanity publishers attempt to disguise their unethical business practices by claiming to be hybrid publishers. However, you should scrutinize the publisher's terms before signing a contract. Will they retain exclusive publishing rights to your book, even if it doesn't sell? Do they demand an enormous upfront fee and expect you to "buy back" unsold copies? Is the company named on a publishing scam watch list? Do they keep a high percentage of your book's profits? Watch out for these red flags as you research your publishing options.

Today, the publishing landscape is undergoing an exciting transformation: the democratization of publishing. Traditionally, publishers served as the gatekeepers of the book world. That is no longer true. It has never been easier to publish a book. With abundant resources, various pathways to publication, and numerous options for authors to share their stories, the process can now be undertaken independently from start to finish in ways never imagined before. While this shift is filled with promise, it's also a lot of work.

Look at it this way. It almost always takes longer to do something independently than with a team around you. This is especially true for writing a book when your background is outside professional writing, editing, and design. The added legwork of doing it on your own often increases the financial, intellectual, and emotional investments—which are *also* much higher when you're flying solo.

In other words, publishing a book alone is not for the faint of heart. We don't want to sugarcoat that fact. We're not saying it can't be done or that it can't be done *well*. But we are dedicated to pulling the curtain aside so you can see what that process looks like and go into it with both eyes open.

We understand if it sounds too overwhelming or you don't have time for it. Most Streamline authors value their time. They know their book is an investment in themselves, their business, and their future. They also find immense value in bringing the right people around their investment to support and grow it. When they see value, they're quick to seize the opportunity.

The Power in Printing

We are motivated to offer our authors Turnkey Publishing—an all-encompassing service represented in our mountain stream graphic from start to finish. If you ask us to name our favorite thing about Turnkey Publishing, it's simple: we get to bring a professional team around your dream.

However, if you ask us what we're *most proud of,* it's our ongoing relationship with authors. We don't just help someone write, edit, and publish their book, only to never speak with them again. On the contrary, we stay connected by helping them get setup with their print on demand accounts and also connect with custom printers who can provide customized print runs and coordinate bulk orders. Advocating for a message you believe in is crucial to getting your book to more people, and quality printing is how we make that message a tangible, viable resource.

THE 10-STEP BOOK PROCESS

1 - IDEATION
2 - OUTLINE
3 - WRITING
4 - EDITING
5 - COVER DESIGN
6 - INTERIOR LAYOUT
7 - PROOFREADING
8 - BOOK LAUNCH
9 - PRINTING
10 - COMMUNITY

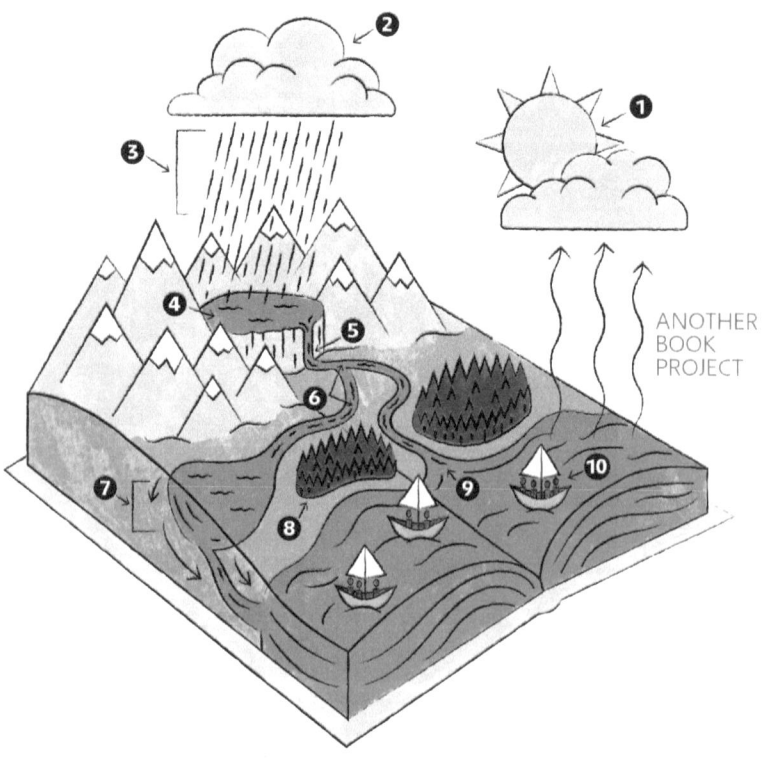

CHAPTER 18

Community

IN OUR MOUNTAIN stream image, the fleet of boats at the end represents a diverse community eagerly awaiting the water that originated from the clouds. Some boats may be grand yachts, while others are humble rowboats, symbolizing people's varied backgrounds and stories. At Streamline, we're dedicated to shifting the perception that book publishing is an individual effort. Instead, we're focused on fostering a vibrant community where authors help each other in a supportive, encouraging forum.

Why Community Matters

It's fun to see men and women on a similar journey, linking arms to navigate the open sea alongside one another. Likewise, it is fulfilling when past, present, and future authors and speakers connect in our community. Social media can connect people from all over the world through their stories. A shared community fosters such connections. However, we know social media has its pitfalls…

- Comparison
- Follower counts
- Fabricated reality
- Time suck
- Sketchy Direct Messages
- Algorithms controlling who can (or cannot) see your content

Whether you have a growing, well-established social media presence or need to learn how to download a social media platform, rest assured social media is *not* community in its truest form. People who make up a community are there for you regardless of online metrics. Community is found in the places you physically gather, like a gym or a church.

Likewise, as an author and speaker, you need a supportive community. Writing a book or sharing your message with the world can be lonely, like being tossed into the middle of the ocean with no help in sight. Picture yourself in the big blue sea, struggling to keep your head above water. Suddenly, you see a boat in the distance slowly sailing towards you. Relief! While the boat offers safety, it's the human connection it represents that you truly crave. *That* is why having a community matters so much. No one should have to navigate the challenges of sharing their message alone when people are ready and willing to support them. You might joke about only getting Amazon reviews from your mom, but others outside your family are eager to help you, too.

Community is Hard

We're faced with the reality day after day: community is hard. It can be *painstakingly* hard at times. When you're flailing about in the ocean, desperately clinging to life, there's at least solace, with no one there to annoy you or say something "off-putting." However, when you finally reach the boat, you aren't sure who you might encounter. It could be just a couple of people, or perhaps there are more than anticipated. Regardless of the number of people, we recognize that any community, regardless of size, has the potential to bring out the best and worst in us.

Living within a community offers opportunities for personal growth. In any communal setting, we share in each other's victories and support one another through challenges. Alongside these shared experiences, we also encounter the quirks and obstacles of fellow community members. Yet, navigating those relationships and differences can foster profound personal development.

It would be best if you did not avoid the community altogether. If a boat comes along offering assistance, please consider accepting their help. While you might scoff at the offer, believing you're managing fine alone, it's worth questioning whether that's true.

Reach up, grab a hand, and get onboard. There's no need to drown in self-doubt alone when support is available. Make a list of all the people in your boat who support you in your journey so that you can share your message with the world. *These* are the individuals worth holding onto. And consider adding Streamline to the top of your list. We'd gladly welcome you in our boat anytime!

THE STREAMLINE PROCESS

CHAPTER 19

Differentiator #1: Our Turnkey Process

STREAMLINE BEGAN ITS journey by distilling the often-years long publishing timeline into an agile, flexible process that produced quality books within a few months. We're incredibly proud of all the books we've published through that method. As our company has grown, our process has evolved to meet the needs of our authors and team members. This evolution has led us to our Turnkey Publishing process.

The fantastic thing is that when we look back on those years of writing, designing, and publishing, it's clear that Turnkey Publishing has always been a part of our journey. Our logo, chosen years ago for its resemblance to the letter "S" and its remove-the-middleman sensibility, fits perfectly. Will loves to say that it's a "cool God thing." That S-shaped logo also resembles

a keyhole, symbolizing our mission to unlock the one-stop shop to bring your book to life.

This applies to a book at any stage. Whether your book needs editing, layout and design, or a ghostwriting service to help you build it from the ground up, we have the services to create a book blueprint and turn it into a finished, turnkey piece of writing ready for the world. We'll bring that team around your dream.

Part of the process includes print-on-demand services. At Streamline, we love this particular gift of technology. In the past, independent authors had to order printed copies of their book in bulk—sometimes thousands of copies—and then find a way to recoup their investment. Traditional publishers often still follow that model. But the beauty of print-on-demand is there's no need for a substantial initial investment. Books are printed as purchased, meaning an author isn't left with a basement full of unsold copies.

Beyond the nuts and bolts of book creation, everything we do is designed to support and encourage our authors through the wild, wonderful, and vulnerable journey of reflection and hard work it takes to bring a book into the world. We want to tell you more about our process, share what sets us apart from other publishers, and give you a peek behind the curtain at what it's like to be a Streamline author. Let's go!

Pre-process:
Building Your Team

WILL

Alex and I firmly believe this is one hundred percent God's business. That's why we dedicate the first twenty to thirty minutes of our Friday morning calls to prayer. From this prayerful foundation, our operations team intentionally matches authors with their writing and editing teams.

There are two main reasons for this intentionality. First, we have a stewardship mindset when helping authors tell their stories. Stewardship involves the responsibility of ensuring your story is told well. We feel that responsibility deeply and treasure the trust you place in us, allowing it to guide everything we do.

Second, we understand the importance of getting the author-team relationship right. Our author's experiences with Streamline show that their working relationships with ghostwriters and editors are genuinely sacred, often becoming the most intimate relationship between two people when stewarding a story. Vulnerability and trust are the oxygen that brings a book to life. We can't take credit for getting it right—as we said, it's God's business, and he guides our choices and matches—but when it does, we're in alignment with Proverbs 31:8, which begins, "Open your mouth for the mute, for the rights of all who are destitute." Our professional writers and editors give voice to authors who aren't quite sure how to commit their stories to paper.

Pre-process:
The Kick-Off Call

ALEX

The first significant milestone for every Streamline author is the Kick-Off Call. These calls are a highlight for us! They remind me of a team meeting in the locker room before a big game—brimming with support and excitement for what's ahead.

During the Kick-Off Call, you'll share your message and why you desire to spread it. For the first time, you'll be surrounded by a team that cares deeply about your message and is dedicated to helping you steward your story. This call is the initial step in defining the scope, message, themes, and principles you'll share in your book. Alongside your writing team, the focus is to build excitement about your book's direction. The clarity that emerges from these meetings is astounding; time and again, we witness incredible breakthroughs from these calls.

Many authors have hidden their book ideas, not sharing them with anyone. The Kick-Off Call provides an opportunity to dive into what you want your book to be about. The call is about vision casting and setting expectations for your book and the journey we're about to embark on together. It's a collaborative meeting between you and your writing/editing team, where we work together to create the book blueprint mentioned earlier. We're passionate about honing in on this blueprint, casting a high-level vision for the audience you want to reach, your book's primary themes, and other guiding elements for the writing process.

Writing a book is like jumping from a plane for the first time. We want to encourage our authors to leap. Doing it with a skilled, professional writing team around you is like making that first jump with an experienced jumper strapped to your back. We want the jump to be mutually beneficial and enjoyable for everyone involved. So, the most important thing an author can do is learn to make a successful jump and prepare accordingly.

The Book Process:
Ghostwriting or Developmental Editing, Design, and Proofreading with Streamline Books

WILL

That brings us to the ghostwriting and developmental editing process. Our goal is to prioritize quality without sacrificing speed. We've assembled a team of expert writers and editors to bring your story to life. They're not skydiving instructors making their first jump—they're seasoned professionals who have made the jump time and time again. We have complete confidence in their abilities because we've witnessed their skill in transforming an author's ideas and stories into compelling, readable, high-quality books. We can't wait to see them bring their expertise to *your* story.

If you've already written your book, we're eager to see our skilled editors sharpen, strengthen, and clarify what's already on the page. Our team of line editors, proofreaders, and interior layout and cover designers will work alongside and behind your ghostwriter or developmental editor to polish and present your book with market-ready finesse. Being in the hands of quality individuals allows you to enjoy the process more and keeps the costs of publishing a book from spiraling out of control.

There's an old saying: buy nice or buy twice. This holds as true in publishing services as it is everywhere else. One of our authors put it best: "If you think hiring excellence is expensive, try hiring an amateur." Just as a hobbyist contractor can throw an entire house off-kilter with one mistake costing thousands of dollars to correct, an inexperienced writer or editor can cost an author thousands of dollars in extra labor to fix problems. At best, these problems result from unskilled labor and good intentions. At worst, they stem from a writing and editing scam. Either way, it takes skilled professionals to review a manuscript and fix what's on the page.

We've personally fielded many manuscripts that have been given the thumbs up by an "editor" the author hired but still need costly work to get them into shape for publication. If this sounds familiar, know that the Streamline team is here to put more than one set of eyes on your book. With multiple checkpoints for quality control, we ensure your book reaches its full potential.

Publishing and Launching Your Book

ALEX

When it comes to publishing and launching your book, there's one thing every author has in common: eventually, they all have to jump. You can do all the preparation, from convincing yourself to skydive to driving to the airfield, walking into the hangar, learning how to pull the lever, suiting up, and boarding the plane. You can strap yourself to an instructor and put your toe to the line. But all that work lacks meaning and impact *unless you jump.*

As authors ourselves, Will and I understand the temptation to go over your book one more time, and one more time, and *one more time*, striving for perfection. But if you continue to chase perfection, you'll miss opportunities to impact lives and bless others with your story. Birds can't fly *until they do.* A baby bird must look over the edge of the nest, gather its courage, spread its wings, and take the leap. When it does, that's when the magic happens.

We've had candid conversations with our authors about this very challenge. The urge to nitpick a manuscript runs deep; we empathize and understand. But remember, when you're a Streamline author, your book has grown up in an entire ecosystem designed to make it the strongest and best it can be. A team of experts has come together around it—and *you*—to prepare it for the world.

To us, that means you can be brave. You did the work. You've earned the leap. Please t*ake it.* Only then can you get to the business of your next book. When you do, our team will be there to help.

A BOOK MAKES YOUR MESSAGE PORTABLE

CHAPTER 20

Differentiator #2: Our Human-Centered Team

BY NOW YOU know the Streamline team comprises professional writers, editors, and designers who are experts in their fields. But there's more to anyone affiliated than just expertise. In the early days of Streamline, we built the foundation of our business on a few core values. Although our values look a little different today, we still believe the following paints a good picture of what you get when working with our team:

> WE SPEAK TRUTH.
> WE BUILD TRUST.
> WE PRIORITIZE COMMUNICATION.
> WE PURSUE EXCELLENCE.
> WE HAVE FUN.

Day to day, we speak the truth when we tell you the world needs your book. We do everything we can to build trust in an industry that can and often does play on peoples' emotions and heartstrings, leading to incredibly exploitative practices. We prioritize communication with our team members, authors, and future authors. You're holding a piece of that vital communication. We pursue the excellence it takes to bring a book to the world and prepare it for the market. In all sorts of ways, we have fun doing all of that.

What does that mean for the people we bring into the Streamline ecosystem? Whether it's writers, editors, designers, or project managers, they already exemplify those core values. We've seen the importance of this over time by partnering with talented people who may not align with our core values. Typically, those partnerships aren't a good fit for either side.

Knowing that we've honed our systems and our team, we're confident that the people our authors will engage with at Streamline are not only top-notch but also living and breathing the core values that are the lifeblood of the Streamline process. When our authors rave about their team, those values come to life.

That means so much to us. As authors, we know what it can be like to wrestle with thoughts and ideas to determine the value of writing a book on our own. Fears and hesitations loom large when they're within the confines of our minds. It's easy to feel lonely and adrift. But that's what's so great about coming into the Streamline ecosystem. Many of our authors talk about how wonderful it is that they aren't alone in the book-writing process. Beginning with the Kick-Off Call, they have a team that is fired up about what they're doing. For some authors, it's the first time they've had that support and encouragement around their book. Let's go!

Pursue Excellence:
Prioritize Talent

WILL

We strive to get the best people in the right seats because we know they can do the jobs of writing, editing, proofreading, and designing better than we can. Entrusting talented individuals is another way we steward our authors' stories. It is also our path to grow and scale so we can help tell even *more* stories and bring more books into the world.

Pursuing excellence is crucial because at Streamline, we know we've never truly "arrived." We love that ethos. Pursuing excellence means we're always striving to get better and grow as a team. We avoid stagnation by wholeheartedly committing to the belief that our efforts will suffer when we take our foot off the gas. That means every time we reach a summit, we survey the mountains in the distance, choose a peak, and ask, "How do we get there?"

Speak Truth:
Right Seats on the Bus

ALEX

Streamline grew out of mutual recognition between Will and me. We were both comfortable in front of groups of people, using our talents to serve others. At the time, Will was onstage more than I was, and then the pendulum swung in the other direction as I tapped into my love of public speaking.

Now, we both get to encourage other people to tell their stories. While God has given us each the ability to be on stage, we find even greater joy in encouraging others in that pursuit and watching them succeed. It's an entirely different rush to play a part in what Streamline is doing and see someone publish their book. It's even more fun.

This value goes back to getting the right people in the right places. We make it our business to create a system of talented teams that care for our authors exceptionally well because each person fills the role they were designed to fill.

Scriptures talk about many members and one body, which perfectly describes teamwork at Streamline. Some people on our team are excellent hands; others are the best feet around. It takes both—and many others—to form a body that communicates effectively and executes the fantastic work of creating a book. We've learned that it's only when people try to function in multiple capacities that they're spread too thin and find themselves in the weeds. When everyone does their part, the process is nearly seamless.

Build Trust:
Culture Keeping

WILL

A while back, I heard a pastor speak about how society is often inclined toward the vast and shallow rather than the narrow and the deep. That idea has stuck with me ever since.

Our process is oriented to the narrow and deep as we walk alongside individuals. We aren't casting the widest net by attempting to work with hundreds or thousands of authors simultaneously because we care about going deep. We recognize it takes an immense amount of trust. Trust is integral to the culture we want to create. We want to genuinely care about you, your story, and your future as an author sharing your message with the world.

Prioritize Communication:
Chief Repeating Officer

WILL

We never want our authors to feel isolated. That's why we prioritize internal communication within our team and active and ongoing communication with our authors. We want them to feel heard and involved throughout the entire process.

Our authors regularly contact their ghostwriters, editors, cover designers, and many other team members. We ensure they feel cared for and heard because silence can breed doubt. In those quiet moments, thoughts like, *"I don't know if this book is good,"* creep in. We've learned that regular encouragement can dispel doubts before they fully form. Streamline's simple culture of affirmation and encouragement is crucial to bringing books like this to readers like you.

That's why I love my job as the Chief Repeating Officer. It's human nature to think, *"Oh, this again,"* when we hear something familiar. But at Streamline, we believe in the power of repetition for essential messages. Phrases like "The world needs your book," "A book makes your message portable," and "The root word of authority is *author*" are worth repeating until they resonate deeply.

This repetition is central to our message. As humans, we often must hear things multiple times before they land. Every day, we are inundated with messages telling us we're not enough or that our story doesn't matter.

Thankfully, we serve a God who understands and loves us. Our Heavenly Father is the ultimate Chief Repeating Officer. He constantly reminds us, "You're my son, my daughter. I love you, and I'm proud of you." Just when we think, *"Yeah, yeah, I've heard that before,"* God doubles down. He reminds us how proud he is of us because we belong to him.

That's the example we strive to follow each day. We aim to repeat these truths until they are heard and embraced because those truths are more significant than we are. By uniting as a team that speaks the truth, we help bring it into the world. We know repeating these truths is necessary. Despite how often we've repeated them, we've seen countless people react as if hearing them for the first time.

THE ROOT WORD OF authority IS *(author)*

CHAPTER 21

Differentiator #3: Our Community

BRINGING A TEAM around your dream is more important than ever. It's a dream that starts with community and ends with our final core value—have fun.

Have Fun

We believe there is no better place to find joy than with a group of like-minded people. That's why we're so proud of the friendships that have been built in our community of authors and speakers that we call The Bestseller Community. Those friendships don't end with your book's publication. Instead, every book published is the beginning of a long-term relationship.

We want to celebrate wins with you—getting copies of your first published book in the mail and landing your first paid speaking engagement. Whatever it is, we want to be with you every step of the way. We hope to make those celebrations and shared resources even more intentional as we continue to grow.

With Streamline, you're part of our author community for life. We hope this relationship will continue to add value to your authorship journey for years after you've launched your book. We want to help you create sustainable, consistent momentum that will be with you once the ink on your book's pages is dry. So, to do that, we want to provide you with resources to create an audiobook, get on a podcast, book a speaking engagement, build a website, create a course, or strategize your marketing. We want to be that catch-all resource to help you make the most of your authorship journey.

We've said it before, and we'll repeat it: The book journey is a marathon, not a sprint. It would be best if you were in it for the long haul to make the most impact. We're here with you in the process. Not to write a bestseller—but to write something *even better* than a bestseller, the book only you were born to write. Someone is counting on you to take action today. Because of that, we can confidently say that the world needs your book.

Where to Go from Here

Our telos (ultimate aim) is to work with value-aligned thought leaders who are looking to impact one person with their story.

When you start with that mindset, you're more likely to enjoy your authorship experience and beyond. Start with that *one* person in mind, just like we mentioned at the beginning of this book, and the book-writing process will feel more like a fun journey than a tiresome slog.

However, there's one more saying we love at Streamline, and it doesn't exactly correlate with a solid sales process—at least not by the normal business world's standards . . .

A Blessing, Not a Burden

In many of our "sales" calls, we convey an important line to anyone thinking about utilizing our services:

"We want our service to be a blessing and not a burden."

We put "sales" in quotes because these calls don't really feel like sales calls at all. Instead, they feel like listening to someone's expertise, passion, and story. Do we have an offering to help them on the other side of that conversation? Absolutely! That's what this section of the book is all about.

On one hand, bringing your book to the world should never be rushed. It's important to take the necessary steps and time to get your manuscript right before hitting *publish*. On the other hand, no human is guaranteed tomorrow. Streamline is somewhere in the middle of those two.

We aim for our service to be a blessing because, without a team like ours, you might go your entire life without capturing your meaningful thoughts and words on paper. We take your time and financial investment very seriously. Often, we meet prospective authors who have been searching for us, even if they didn't know we existed.

But we do exist! And so does an audience eager to read and hear your words. If you have any doubts, you're not alone—many of us are our own worst critics.

"Who would want to listen to what I have to say?"

As we mentioned in Chapter 6, you have seeds to plant in the minds and hearts of more people than you realize. A book can be the starting point, and who knows where it might lead. Trust us, it's a daunting journey, but one worth taking. Those seeds are likely to sprout life in unexpected places.

It all starts with an idea. With a little rain, groundflow, and cultivation, your words come to life—bringing your story to the world.

AFTERWORD (LET'S GO!)

ALTHOUGH MANY ASSOCIATE the term "Let's go!" with Tom Brady, known as "The GOAT" of NFL quarterbacks, it's worth noting that this book was authored by two Chiefs fans.

So, when we shout "Let's go!" alongside our Streamline authors, we probably have another 'GOAT' in mind: Patrick Mahomes. Regardless of your football allegiance, we love working with all kinds of football fans– even those who have never watched a single snap.

To you, we say LET'S GO! If you're ready to put this book down and start writing your own, simply visit our website using the QR code on the following page. We'd love to

1. Hear your story and
2. Help you share it with the world!

We want everything about working with our team to be a blessing, while helping you achieve your dream of bringing your book to life. Tomorrow isn't guaranteed, so scan that QR code today. Who knows where this one decision could lead? One thing is for sure—we can't wait to find out.

"Let's go!"

—WILL SEVERNS and ALEX DEMCZAK

 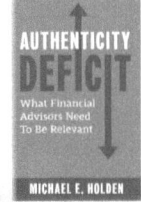  

 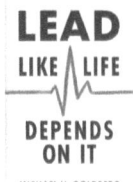  

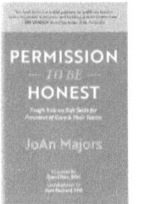   

writemybooks.com

THE World NEEDS Your Book

www.ingramcontent.com/pod-product-compliance
Lightning Source LLC
Chambersburg PA
CBHW020241010526
44107CB00039B/1458/J